INTEGRATING INQUIRY IN SOCIAL STUDIES CLASSROOMS

D1500574

This practical guide shows how and why in-service and pre-service teachers should use inquiry in their social studies lessons to develop students' critical thinking and decision-making skills. Supported by literature and research, it provides a concrete framework for integrating inquiry in the classroom, which outlines the pedagogical practice of inquiry and provides evidence for its benefits for teaching and learning.

Filled with practical advice and lesson plans for classroom use, chapters explore topics such as the following:

- Defining inquiry and highlighting its importance in the classroom;
- An overview of the inquiry framework and the role of pedagogical content knowledge;
- The literature and research about inquiry, including alternate framework structures and the different types of inquiry; and
- Planning and scaffolding inquiry-based learning.

The volume also explores perennial and emerging uses for inquiry in social studies, including technology, integrating literature, utilizing civic agency, using primary sources, evaluating sources, and focusing on global issues.

This is an essential read for any pre-service or in-service teacher who wants to support their students in developing inquiry skills.

Carolyn A. Weber is an associate professor at the University of Northern Iowa.

Heather N. Hagan is an associate professor at Coastal Carolina University.

'We live in an age in which we must be dedicated to teaching children how to engage in authentic inquiry. Authentic inquiry teaches students to think critically, to deliberate democratically, and prepares students for participatory democracy. This book provides a clear framework for teachers to use to achieve this goal.'

Dr. Dean P. Vesperman, *Assistant Professor of Education at the University of Wisconsin River Falls*

INTEGRATING INQUIRY IN SOCIAL STUDIES CLASSROOMS

Carolyn A. Weber and
Heather N. Hagan

NEW YORK AND LONDON

Designed cover image: dv1940060 / Getty Images

First published 2024
by Routledge
605 Third Avenue, New York, NY 10158

and by Routledge
4 Park Square, Milton Park, Abingdon, Oxon, OX14 4RN

Routledge is an imprint of the Taylor & Francis Group, an informa business

© 2024 Carolyn A. Weber and Heather N. Hagan

Library of Congress Cataloging-in-Publication Data
Names: Weber, Carolyn A., author. | Hagan, Heather N., author.
Title: Integrating inquiry in social studies classrooms / Carolyn A. Weber, Heather N. Hagan.
Description: New York : Routledge, 2023. | Includes bibliographical references and index.
Identifiers: LCCN 2022061184 (print) | LCCN 2022061185 (ebook) | ISBN 9781032227818 (hbk) | ISBN 9781032227818 (pbk) | ISBN 9781003274148 (ebk)
Subjects: LCSH: Inquiry-based learning. | Social sciences—Study and teaching. | Critical thinking. | Decision making. | Problem solving.
Classification: LCC LB1027.23 .W43 2023 (print) | LCC LB1027.23 (ebook) | DDC 372.89—dc23/eng/20230331
LC record available at https://lccn.loc.gov/2022061184
LC ebook record available at https://lccn.loc.gov/2022061185

ISBN: 978-1-032-22783-2 (hbk)
ISBN: 978-1-032-22781-8 (pbk)
ISBN: 978-1-003-27414-8 (ebk)

DOI: 10.4324/9781003274148

Typeset in Joanna
by Apex CoVantage, LLC

Dedicated to Terry, Lee, Ellarose, Mark, Tyler, and Henry.

CONTENTS

ACKNOWLEDGEMENTS

The idea for this book began in graduate school. After several presentations and much work together about inquiry-based learning, we planned to eventually write a book when we both earned tenure. Now, about a decade later, here we are. Over those years, we have had the privilege to work with countless teachers and scholars who have helped us refine our ideas. We want to thank the faculty and alumni of Indiana University's Department of Curriculum and Instruction. IU was the birthplace of our framework, and our colleagues there inspired and fostered much of our work. Specifically, we would like to thank Keith C. Barton, Lynne Boyle-Baise, and Leanna McClain for their invaluable mentorship.

Additionally, we want to specifically thank Katelyn Browne and the staff at UNI's Rod Library for helping to identify children's books for the Chapter 6 highlighted lesson. We are also grateful for the scholars and teachers who have supported this work — giving feedback in presentations, welcoming us into their classrooms, and building the foundation for our field. It was also a pleasure to work with our editors, Matthew Friberg and Emmie Shand, and the staff at Routledge.

Finally, we would like to thank our husbands, Terry Duncan and Mark Hagan. They picked up the slack, provided incredible emotional support, and listened to us drone on about inquiry. We could not have finished this book without their help.

PART I

INTRODUCTION TO INQUIRY

This book supports both in-service and pre-service teachers with a general introduction to and evidence for using inquiry in their social studies lessons. The bulk of this book, though, focuses on a framework that is written to support teachers and students as they design and conduct inquiry. We argue that the ultimate goal of including inquiry in the social studies classroom is to develop students' critical thinking and decision-making skills as educated citizens. Therefore, a primary tenet is to equip teachers to scaffold students as they develop their own inquiries.

This book is divided into two sections. Part one is divided into four chapters. The first chapter focuses on defining inquiry, including the historical calls for inquiry, how inquiry is used in other content areas, a brief overview of our framework, and the importance of teaching with inquiry. We also discuss the role of pedagogical content knowledge in inquiry-based teaching and as a structure for our framework.

DOI: 10.4324/9781003274148-1

Chapter 2 focuses on the literature and research about inquiry. We begin with a survey of recently published inquiries. Then we discuss some common structures of inquiry frameworks and disagreements about the necessary elements of an inquiry. After that, we discuss different types of inquiries. Finally, we end Chapter 2 with a discussion of the support teachers need to create inquiry lessons.

Chapter 3 is where we really delve into our framework, providing a detailed overview of the pedagogical aspect of inquiry design. In this chapter, we elaborate on each aspect of our framework. We also include how it is adaptable for various grade levels and student needs and even for different types of inquiries.

Chapter 4 is the last chapter in the first section of this book. It is devoted to addressing teacher's content knowledge for planning successful inquiries. In this chapter, we offer a range of suggestions about where teachers can find reliable resources. Finally, we end this chapter with a discussion about how to scaffold inquiry, particularly source-discovery and evaluation within inquiry, for students' independence in designing inquiries.

1

WHAT IS INQUIRY AND WHY SHOULD WE TEACH IT?

On a typical day, the average person "googles" something about 3–4 times, and in 2022, there were about 3.5 billion Google searches every day (Google Search Statistics, n.d.). Almost everyone can find information at any moment on their smartphone or another device. For the field of social studies education, this could be a dream come true. After all, the National Council for the Social Studies (NCSS) states, "The primary purpose of social studies is to help young people develop the ability to make informed and reasoned decisions for the public good as citizens of a culturally diverse, democratic society in an interdependent world," (About National Council for the Social Studies, n.d.). However, social studies educators know that becoming citizens who can make "informed and reasoned decisions for the public good" requires more than a simple Google search. Citizens must be able to ask the right questions; use their background knowledge to understand what they hear, read, and see; gather and evaluate evidence; consider multiple perspectives; and

DOI: 10.4324/9781003274148-2

look beyond themselves to the needs of the larger community. Although evidence and support may be "googled," these vital citizenship skills cannot be achieved so simply.

We believe that inquiry can prepare the active, informed citizens described by NCSS (About National Council for the Social Studies, n.d.). Inquiry is a student-centered teaching strategy that allows students an opportunity to grapple with hard questions and eventually ask their own difficult questions. It teaches students how to find and evaluate sources and can initiate action to address complicated problems. In short, inquiry helps students to develop critical thinking skills through asking questions, researching evidence, revising thinking, and reaching conclusions based on evidence. It prepares our citizens to go beyond "googling."

History of Inquiry

Inquiry is not a new concept within education. In the late 1800s, German educators began to push for students to use primary sources to "construct their own historical accounts" in an early form of inquiry (Thornton, 2001, p. 192). In the United States, Dewey (1910, 2011) became an advocate of inquiry as part of reflective teaching. He wrote that "to carry on systematic and protracted inquiry – these are the essentials of thinking" (Dewey, 1910, 2011, p. 13). He argued that it was education's job to help students "cultivate deep-seated and effective habits of discriminating tested beliefs from mere assertions, guesses, and opinions" (Dewey, 1910, 2011, pp. 27–28). Early progressive education focused on students using inquiry and primary sources to develop critical thinking skills – to move beyond rote memorization and think more deeply about the topics they are learning about.

While calls for the inclusion of inquiry go back as far as the 1800s, Barton and Levstik (2004) argue that the evidence of inquiry's implementation in schools is less common. Because research into early social studies focused primarily on national publications and the work of specific scholars, there are gaps in the literature (Woyshner, 2009). For example, after analyzing the textbooks for Home Geography courses from the early twentieth century, Barton (2009) argues that the textbooks and lack of teacher training led to a superficial teaching of Home Geography, which then led to students learning about the social world but not in the way reformers of the day intended. Whether inquiry was not taught or just taught superficially after Dewey's recommendations remains unclear; however, what is clear is that every generation of reformers continues to recommend inquiry as a social studies strategy again and again. For example, the New Social Studies of the 1960s also called for inquiry to be used. Fenton (1967) argued that students need to practice inquiry in order to develop critical thinking skills. He also defined six steps to inquiry: 1. "Recognizing a problem from data" 2. "Formulating hypothesis" 3. "Recognizing the logical implications of hypotheses" 4. "Gathering data" 5. "Analyzing, evaluating, and interpreting data" and 6. "Evaluating the hypothesis in light of the data" (pp. 16–17). His steps are similar to Dewey's, but again, even though inquiry was recommended in the 1910s and 1960s, little evidence exists to show that it was widely implemented. Many of the progressive ideas of the 1960s were later challenged in the cultural wars of the 1970s and 1980s (Weber et al., 2010).

50 years after the New Social Studies, in 2013, NCSS published *Social Studies for the Next Generation: Purposes, Practices, and Implications of the College, Career, and Civic Life (C3) Framework for Social Studies State Standards*, which also called for the use of inquiry to teach social studies. The C3 framework describes the inquiry arc as "a set of interlocking and mutually supportive ideas that frame the ways students learn Social Studies content." It continues, "by focusing on inquiry, the framework emphasizes the disciplinary concepts and practices that support students as they develop the capacity to know, analyze, explain, and argue about interdisciplinary challenges in our social world" (p. 6). While Dewey (1910, 2011) and Fenton (1967) included writing and revising hypotheses in their inquiry recommendations, the C3 framework and others (Levstik & Barton, 2022) removed this aspect. Our framework, explained generally later and in more detail in Chapter 3, reinstates the use of hypotheses into inquiry.

A significant difference between when Dewey (1910, 2011) and Fenton (1967) called for the use of inquiry in social studies education and when the C3 framework repeated the recommendation is the development of state standards. The C3 framework has been used by 32 states to model their own standards, including the development of an inquiry arc or inquiry-specific standards (New et al., 2021). After the development of the C3 framework, Swan et al. (2018) published the *Inquiry Design Model* (IDM). In this book, they go through their framework for how teachers can write inquiry lesson plans and provide examples. Since its publishing, several more articles have been published with lessons using IDM for the foundation of inquiry and online databases for IDM lessons are being developed. With the adoption of the C3 framework in state standards and the publications of the IDM and lessons, which follow the IDM, inquiry may finally become more than just a recommendation for teaching social studies. However, even with inquiry as part of the standards, teachers can still avoid teaching inquiry or may teach it superficially, just like Barton's (2009) Home Geography example. One of the authors, for example, completed an inquiry about the standards with her elementary pre-service teachers. The compelling question was "Do our state's social studies standards promote the use of inquiry to teach social studies?" Almost across the board, her students commented that the standards uphold inquiry, but most of them could be taught with more "traditional" methods. With this book, we hope to make inquiry teaching more accessible and compelling for current and future social studies teachers.

Across Content Areas

Inquiry, as an educational strategy, is not limited to social studies. During the New Social Studies era, Fenton (1967) wrote, "Teachers in every field share responsibility for teaching the skills of inquiry" (p. 11). Even though inquiry has been recommended in multiple disciplines, it is probably better known in science education more than any other discipline (Lakin & Wallace, 2015; Akuma & Callaghan, 2019; Wallace & Coffey, 2019). In science education, inquiry can be defined as "students using knowledge, reasoning, and skills to conduct investigations much like scientists would" (Lakin & Wallace, 2015). With a focus on doing science in the Next Generation Science Standards, inquiry can be utilized through experiments and research.

Similarly, inquiry has even been used in order to integrate science and literacy. Wallace and Coffey (2019) found that when pre-service teachers were encouraged to teach science and literacy together, many used aspects of inquiry, even though it was not required. The pre-service teachers wrote units in which students practiced skills, such as "making claims and finding evidence, looking for and finding patterns in data, and, in a few instances, making cause-and-effect explanations" (Wallace & Coffey, 2019, p. 522). All of these skills are aspects of inquiry-based instruction. By utilizing these inquiry aspects in units, which integrated literacy and science, students improved both their literacy and science skills.

While inquiry might be more well known in science, inquiry-based instruction is also used in math education (Hahkloniemi, 2017; Von Renesse & Ecke, 2017). In math education, inquiry is defined slightly differently from how it is defined within science education. Hahkloniemi (2017) wrote, "In inquiry-based mathematics teaching, students work alone or in small groups to solve non-standard mathematical problems designed to potentially bring forth mathematical ideas related to the topic at hand" (p. 5). They continued, "the teacher supports the students in their reasoning and orchestrates classroom discussion" (p. 6). Similarly, Von Renesse and Ecke (2017) argue the importance of using inquiry-based instruction in math. They say that when a teacher develops a "culture of asking questions," then students gain curiosity and begin to ask their own questions (p. 159). Inquiry, as Dewey (1910, 2011) and Fenton (1967) note, is an integral part of teaching students how to think critically, no matter the content area.

While our focus is on social studies, students may come with prior knowledge or assumptions about inquiry from other subject areas. We have had students question the use of inquiry in social studies because "inquiry belongs in science" or "I've only ever heard of inquiry in science classes." This book is our response to those implied questions. In it, we lay out how inquiry can, and should, be an integral part of social studies classrooms from kindergarten through middle school. Preschoolers and high schoolers can and should be involved in inquiry, too, and although those ages are not the focus of this book, the skills and lessons we lay out can be tweaked to fit their needs.

Our Framework

Our conception of inquiry is built around Dewey's concept of reflective thought (Dewey, 1910, 2011; Barton & Levstik, 2004). Individuals begin to wonder about something and ask questions. Then, based on their prior knowledge and experiences, they propose a hypothesis. However, they must seek further information to solve their problem or answer their question, so they gather and evaluate evidence. Finally, based on their evidence, they are able to reach a conclusion.

Inquiry builds critical thinking skills, which are crucial for our democracy (Barton & Levstik, 2004; Parker, 2005). As mentioned earlier, one role of schools is to educate and prepare citizens for their roles as active participants in our democratic society. But that raises the question as to what skills citizens need. Ochoa-Becker (2007) advocates that students best learn citizenship through an issues-centered decision-making curriculum. Common social studies skills, she wrote, are not enough. In a curriculum designed to educate for democratic citizenship, instruction should focus "on applying the intellect to make meaning to enhance understanding, to expand comprehension and to support decision making and political action that can make democracy stronger." She goes on to list a few intellectual abilities strong student-citizens should develop (pp. 53–56):

1. Being able to identify complex issues and cast them in a broad perspective, identifying points of controversy as well as the underlying values which may be in conflict.
2. Being able to select and access relevant information about the issue from a variety of fields of study and from sources that present competing and contrasting points of view.
3. Being able to create a future scenario of likely consequences regarding any proposed solution to an issue and to identify the criteria (values) by which these consequences should be judged.
4. Being able to make reasoned judgments where the evidence is conflicting or where there is a conflict of values.
5. Being able to understand the perspectives of people who hold different views or different cultural perspectives regarding an issue. What reasons and/or what evidence support their conclusions? Do these reasons or this evidence deserve consideration?
6. Being able to choose or create a solution which, though less than ideal, is politically viable and moves in the desired direction.

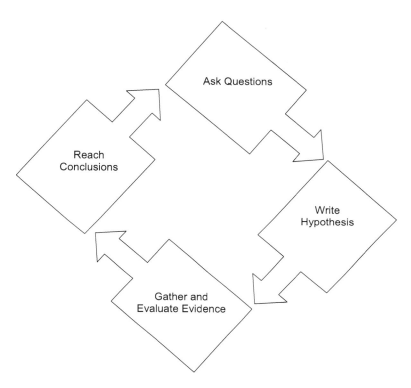

Figure 1.1 The cycle of inquiry

We believe that inquiry-based learning develops these intellectual abilities in our students. Whether asking questions or identifying issues to explore, the goal is to identify controversies, issues, and values that are intriguing or troublesome and then turn those into questions. Developing those questions into inquiries then allows students the opportunity to practice and develop the intellectual abilities of a strong student-citizen. Inquiry calls for students to examine multiple perspectives, varying opinions, and the democratic values at play. They must use and refine their disciplinary knowledge through supported analysis and evaluation of resources, and their findings then provide evidence for their conclusions. In all of these steps, skillful teachers facilitate student questioning and ensure that they are analyzing the perspectives and conclusions of others. Finally, student conclusions are weighed and evaluated as they decide the next steps towards community action or sharing their learning with others. As students strengthen these citizenship and inquiry skills, teachers can gradually withdraw support and facilitate independent student inquiry.

One aspect of our framework is that it guides students to develop their own inquiries. In each example, we discuss where and how teachers can withdraw support and scaffolding in order for students to be more in control of the inquiries. These chapters are mostly written to be used as-is for intermediate grades. However, we include how they can be adapted for younger AND older children, including how to release the teacher's control of the inquiry and give it to students. Also, within our detailed description of the process in Chapter 3, we address how students can create their own inquiries or merely portions of the inquiry, such as students writing the questions but the teacher helping to find sources. Or the teacher asks the questions, but the students complete the research to answer the questions. Eventually, the students should be able to fully initiate and lead the inquiry process.

Teaching Inquiry

This book serves as a guide for developing inquiry lessons or units using this framework. Developing inquiry-based instruction requires teachers to combine specific content knowledge and a particular method into pedagogical content knowledge (PCK). PCK is probably the most crucial step for developing an inquiry, and it changes each time we develop a new inquiry lesson. PCK, as explained by Shulman (1987), takes what teachers know about the content and pedagogy, in this case inquiry, to create a professional understanding of what teachers need to know and do to be able to teach the content in a way that best suits the needs of that class of students. Teachers need to both know the content and how students will learn the content. They must fuse the content into the pedagogy by understanding the topic and also understanding how students need the topic to be organized and represented. PCK is where educators' expertise lies, in the blending of content and the methods best suited to teach it.

When we analyze the PCK needed to teach social studies through inquiry, there are two components that must be developed: content knowledge and pedagogy. In each example in this book, we provide information about how to develop content knowledge about the topic for both teachers and students and then how to turn the content knowledge into an inquiry, thus creating PCK.

The process of inquiry is at the heart of this book. Our framework supports teachers' pedagogical practice, presents a method well-suited and adaptable for student learning, and includes several examples that can be adapted between grade levels and for differing abilities. The process to develop inquiry lessons using this framework is detailed in Chapter 3, so we will not focus much on it here. However, it is important for us to acknowledge that the framework and content knowledge is simply a portion of the PCK teachers need to implement. Each chapter will equip teachers with some basic content knowledge and a lesson plan, but we know that teaching is more than that. We trust educators' knowledge of their students' and classrooms' needs and realize the importance of their professional judgment in adjusting their practice to best support their context, which is where the true magic happens.

Conclusion

This process outlined earlier might remind you of the scientific process and it is, indeed, similar. However, the skills and process can be the same across disciplines because it represents the essence of critical thinking, not only of scientific thinking (Barton & Levstik, 2004; Parker, 2005). It is this type of critical thinking that builds the foundation for citizenship.

Though inquiry can be carried throughout the school subjects, it fits well within social studies instruction. The National Council for Social Studies (NCSS) defines social studies as the following:

> Social studies is the integrated study of the social sciences and humanities to promote civic competence. . . . The primary purpose of social studies is to help young people develop the ability to make informed and reasoned decisions for the public good as citizens of a culturally diverse, democratic society in an interdependent world.
>
> (About National Council for the Social Studies, n.d.)

The purpose of social studies is to educate citizens. Oftentimes, we consider social studies as history or geography lessons. In elementary schools, we know that social studies is frequently shoved to the back burner (Boyle-Baise et al., 2008). But if social studies education is to educate *future citizens*, instruction needs to move beyond reading and outlining chapters, defining vocabulary, answering textbook questions, and listening to lectures. Citizens must be able to "make informed and reasoned decisions for the public good" (About National Council for the Social Studies, n.d.). Furthermore, they must also realize that this public includes the differing viewpoints, perspectives, and needs of a "culturally diverse, democratic society in an interdependent world" (About National Council for the Social Studies, n.d.). Inquiry facilitates the development of critical thinking skills and the evaluation of differing perspectives in order to change the world around us.

We will delve more deeply into the framework's rationale and specific connections to citizenship in Chapter 3. However, inquiry, regardless of the framework, seeks to answer questions and grapple with issues and values. As mentioned earlier, it builds critical thinking, which is crucial as we prepare students for democratic participation and is exactly why we felt compelled to write this book. Parker (2005) contrasts the concept of a citizen with that of an idiot. An idiot, according to the original Greek, is someone concerned with themselves, who is selfish, and focused on their private life. They seek their own liberty at all costs without seeing that their liberty comes from the protection of the community. A citizen, on the other hand, is concerned with the public, common good. The citizen is knowledgeable and engaged in building a diverse community. Inquiry, we believe, is well-suited to developing our students into citizens.

References

About National Council for the Social Studies. (n.d.). *National council for the social studies.* Retrieved November 7, 2022, from www.socialstudies.org/about

Akuma, F. V., & Callaghan, R. (2019). Teaching practices linked to the implementation of inquiry-based practical work in certain science classrooms. *Journal of Research in Science Teaching, 56,* 64–90. https://doi.org/10.1002/tea.21469

Barton, K. C. (2009). Home geography and the development of elementary social education, 1890–1930. *Theory & Research in Social Education, 37*(4), 484–514. https://doi.org/10.1080/00933104.2009.10473408

Barton, K. C., & Levstik, L. S. (2004). *Teaching history for the common good.* (6th ed). Routledge.

Boyle-Baise, M., Hsu, M. C., Johnson, S., Serriere, S. C., & Stewart, D. (2008). Putting reading first: Teaching social studies in elementary classrooms. *Theory & Research in Social Education, 36*(3), 233–255. https://doi.org/10.1080/00933104.2008.10473374

Dewey, J. (2011). *How we think.* Project Gutenberg. (Original work published 1910).

Fenton, E. (1967). *The new social studies.* Holt, Rinehart, & Winston, Inc.

Google Search Statistics. (n.d.). *Internet live stats.* Retrieved November 7, 2022, from www.internetlivestats.com/google-search-statistics/

Hahkloniemi, M. (2017). Student teachers' types of probing questions in inquiry-based mathematics teaching with and without GeoGebra. *International Journal of Mathematical Education in Science and Technology, 48*(7), 973–987. https://doi.org/10.1080/0020739X.2017.1329558

Lakin, J. M., & Wallace, C. S. (2015). Assessing dimensions of inquiry practice by middle school science teachers engaged in a professional development program. *Journal of Science Teacher Education, 26,* 139–162. https://doi.org/10.1007/s10972-014-9412-1

Levstik, L. S., & Barton, K. C. (2022). *Doing history: Investigating with children in elementary and middle school.* Routledge. https://doi.org/10.4324/9781003179658

National Council for the Social Studies. (2013). *Social studies for the next generation: Purposes, practices, and implications of the college, career, and civic life (C3) framework for social studies state standard.* NCSS Publications. www.socialstudies.org/sites/default/files/c3/c3-framework-for-social-studies-revo617.pdf

New, R., Swan, K., Lee, J., & Grant, S. G. (2021). The state of social studies standards: What is the impact of the C3 framework? *Social Education, 85*(4), 239–246.

Ochoa-Becker, A. S. (2007). *Democratic education for social studies an issues-centered decision making curriculum* (2nd ed.). IAP-Information Age Pub.

Parker, W. (2005). *Social studies in elementary education* (12th ed.). Pearson Merrill/Prentice Hall.

Shulman, L. (1987). Knowledge and teaching: Foundations of the new reform. *Harvard Educational Review*, 57(1), 1–23. https://doi.org/10.17763/haer.57.1.j463w79r56455411

Swan, K., Lee, J., & Grant, S. G. (2018). *Inquiry design model: Building inquiries in social studies*. National Council for the Social Studies.

Thornton, S. J. (2001). Legitimacy in the social studies curriculum. In L. Corno (Ed.), *Education across a century: The centennial volume. One hundredth yearbook of the national society for the study of education, part 1.* The University of Chicago Press.

Von Renesse, C., & Ecke, V. (2017). Teaching inquiry with a lens toward curiosity. *PRIMUS*, 27(1), 148–164. https://doi.org/10.1080/10511970.2016.1176973

Wallace, C. S., & Coffey, D. J. (2019). Investigating elementary preservice teachers' designs for integrated science/literacy instruction highlighting similar cognitive processes. *Journal of Science Teacher Education*, 30(5), 507–527. https://doi.org/10.1080/1046560X.2019.1587569

Weber, C. A., Frye, J. M., Ables, C., & Goodman, J. (2010). Curriculum and the 1970s culture wars: Man a course of study. *Curriculum History*, 40–59.

Woyshner, C. (2009). Introduction: Histories of social studies thought and practice in schools and communities. *Theory & Research in Social Education*, 37(4), 426–431. https://doi.org/10.1080/00933104.2009.10473405

2

WHAT DOES THE RESEARCH
SAY ABOUT INQUIRY?

This chapter provides a literature review over recent designs and uses of inquiry. We delve into controversies surrounding different formats and disagreements about elements within inquiry. We focus on the different types of inquiry and include a survey of recently published inquiries in social studies and literacy journals. Finally, we address the support teachers need to be able to teach with inquiry.

Survey of Recent Published Inquiries

Inquiry has enjoyed a bit of a renaissance in recent years due to the publication of the National Council for the Social Studies' college, career, and civic life (C3) framework (2013). There is currently a plethora of inquiry-related practitioner articles in journals, such as *Social Studies and the Young Learner*, *The Social Studies*, *Middle Level Learning*, and *Social Education*. For the purpose of this literature review, we focused on articles published

DOI: 10.4324/9781003274148-3

since 2018 in these social studies journals and a few non–social studies journals. We looked at inquiry broadly and chose to highlight lessons and units, which the authors and editors described as inquiry. Because the C3 framework is so broad, many inquiries that cite it are very unique. The focus of the articles is rarely how to design an inquiry or how to help students design an inquiry but tend to showcase one or two areas of inquiry. The inquiries that have been published primarily focus on the sources used, ways to integrate literacy, or how to include different levels of structure.

Several of the articles highlight their use of primary sources within inquiry lessons or units. Mehta (2022) writes about using digital archives to find primary sources to use in an inquiry about early South Asian American history. They reference the C3 framework, but it is very different from Muetterties et al. (2020), who also reference the C3 framework. Muetterties et al. (2020) focus also on using primary sources on their inquiry about voting, but they limit the inquiry to just looking at the question, tasks, and sources. Similarly, Muetterties and Haney (2018) wrote an inquiry about local history. While their questions (and even some of their sources) are universal, the students focused on the local history of slavery. All of these articles feature the use of primary sources. Mehta (2022) and Muetterties et al. (2020) follow the C3 framework broadly, while Muetterties and Haney (2018) are more specific in their inquiry design.

Arguably, the focus on sources can also be considered a focus on content over process. Shear et al. (2018) connect a lesson about affirming Indigenous sovereignty to the C3 framework, but the content seems more important than the inquiry process. In contrast, Payne and Green (2018) focus on aspects of the process in that they write about how to prepare students for historical perspective recognition through an early inquiry into students' identity and perspectives. They briefly mention a historical inquiry in which students used what they learned in the identify inquiry to recognize the perspective of others.

A subset of inquiry lessons recently published focuses on the integration of literature. Inquiry is a good way to bring both literature and social studies standards into an elementary classroom as we discuss in Chapter 6. Kucan et al. (2019), Hubbard et al. (2021), and Brugar (2019) all discuss how to integrate literacy and social studies within inquiry. Kucan et al. (2019) focus on literacy and do not reference either C3 or IDM. They created problem-based inquiry as part of their literature research, but the focus was on local history, and they worked with social studies teachers. Brugar (2019), while still focusing on literacy, takes a different path. She uses a trade book as a model for how historians use inquiry. She explains how the book fits into the C3 framework as an example of doing history.

One interesting part of the lessons we surveyed for this book is the different levels of structure involved. For example, Casey et al. (2019) completed an inquiry with preschool students, but it was a very open-ended inquiry. They focused on "unplanned, spontaneous inquiry" (p. 2), allowing the students questions to guide their inquiry within a unit on gardening. In contrast, Wargo and Alvarado (2020) also wrote about a preschool inquiry, but it was much more structured. They used the C3 framework as a basis of an inquiry about community with three-year-old children. Similarly, Kim and Falkner (2022) meticulously plan their unit on Asian American history, designing several stations, which each focused on a different event in Asian American history. Because the C3 framework is so broad, each lesson or unit based on it can be planned with as little or as much structure as meets the students' and teachers' needs.

This review shows that inquiry is a popular method in current research, but the focus is varied. Studies are not always on how to plan an inquiry. Instead, the focus might be on a single facet of the content or process. Taken as a whole, this literature shows that there is plenty of more work to be done because the inquiry format itself does not have to fit every classroom. But instead, both the content and process can be modified to fit instructional needs.

Structures and Forms of Inquiry

It is not surprising that the literature reviewed shows the teachers shape inquiry to meet their needs, as there are various formats of inquiry in the field of education. The scientific method, which some say originated in the 1600s (Betz, 2011), is at the root of many inquiry formats, including the one we provide in this book. It outlines the sequence of steps in the scientific inquiry process and, in its simplest form, includes scientists asking questions, making a hypothesis, investigating, and drawing conclusions. However, the "scientific method" is also being questioned (Bobrowsky, 2021; Cutraro, 2012). Though taught in schools, some argue that it's not how scientists really investigate in the real-world. Science does not follow a clean, tidy process of the same sequence of steps in every investigation. Bobrowsky (2021) says that, in the real-world:

> Scientists ask questions about anything in the world (or universe) and then look for pathways to answers. After finding out what's already known about the topic, they get more information in a variety of ways – by making observations, by undertaking scientific experiments/investigations, and by making calculations. So, there's not a single "method;" there are many scientific methods.
>
> (p. 89, emphasis original)

Considering scientific inquiry as asking and answering questions using a variety of methods fits with our experiences solving problems in the real-world. Scientists do not find information and answer questions using the same set of steps. However, the scientific method can be a useful tool for teachers. It can be helpful to students to have a guided approach when learning how to engage in scientific inquiry. At the same time, there does not need to be a one-size-fits-all approach. The scientific method can be a starting point, but students can, and should, develop a more robust set of problem-solving skills and tools in order to answer their questions. The scientific method, and any inquiry framework, can be a foundation for learning inquiry, but ultimately, the instructional goal is for students to be able to inquire and problem-solve on their own.

Considering the discussion about the scientific method's narrow approach to inquiry, it is not surprising that approaches to social studies inquiry vary. Amongst practitioners and researchers engaging students in social studies inquiry, there are various approaches and formats, some even coming from science education. While a few have been widely adopted, others were used merely for the scope of an instructional unit or research study.

One model, which began in science, is the 5E instructional model that was originally proposed as a part of the Science for Life and Living elementary program (Bybee & Landes, 1990). This inquiry model is still popular in science and has been used in social studies instruction, albeit less widely. Based on constructivist principles, there are five steps. Notably, answering questions, not asking questions, is the focus of this framework; however, the observation of the environment will often be the trigger for questioning. The first phase, Engagement is when teachers support student connections to background knowledge, introduce the topic or concept, and may ask questions. Exploration follows, and students engage in common experiences where they actively explore and observe their environment and work with materials. Then in the Explanation phase, students and teachers review their experience. Teachers will ask students about their understanding and might focus student attention on a particular aspect of the exploration. This phase might also formally introduce concepts, definitions, skills, or labels. Next, in the Elaboration phase, students extend their learning to develop broader conceptual understandings or practice skills. Finally, the Evaluation phase is a chance for students and teachers to assess understanding and evaluate progress towards learning objectives. Since its introduction, this model has been popular in science education but is not the only one.

Another framework for inquiry in science that has also had an impact in social studies is claims, evidence, reasoning, rebuttal (CERR) (McNeill & Martin, 2011), and similar to 5E, this framework focuses on answering questions rather than asking them. Initially, students make a claim to address a question or problem. Then they gather evidence to support that claim. This evidence might come from direct observations or research. Then students explain how and why the evidence supports their claim in the Reasoning phase. The final phase, Rebuttal, is not usually introduced until students are familiar with C-E-R, which is often in middle or high school.

Not all inquiry frameworks began in science, though. Boyle-Baise and Zevin (2009), for example, created the "Design for Inquiry" lesson plan format. After engaging student interest, the teacher raises an essential question and elicits a hypothesis or "good guess" (pp. 245–246) as a class and individually. After that, students examine one data set at a time and revise the hypothesis on the board in between each. Then they revise their personal hypothesis. Finally, they write and share their conclusions. Additionally, to motivate students, Boyle-Baise and Zevin advocate approaching inquiry as a detective, where each source is viewed as a clue and students work to solve the case.

In 2013, the National Council for the Social Studies published their college, career, and civic life (C3) framework. This has directed much of the social studies inquiry since its publication and laid the foundation for the inquiry design model (IDM), which appears to be the model of choice amongst NCSS and many of the state social studies councils

NCSS's C3 framework (2013) is designed to guide states in developing robust, inquiry-based standards and, also, to support practitioners as the engage in inquiry-based instruction

It is tied closely to the Common Core standards and supports state standards, which facilitates student questioning, uses the disciplines as tools, and identifies evidence, which supports their conclusions. But citizenship does not stop there. Citizenship requires that inquirers ask tough questions and use their conclusions to spark change. Citizenship also requires that they continue to ask those questions again and again.

Additionally, the C3 framework is designed around the inquiry arc, a model that takes students and teachers through inquiry steps to support college, career, and civic life. The arc has four dimensions:

1. **Developing questions and planning inquiries:** This dimension entails writing both compelling questions, which represent key ideas and concepts, and supporting questions, which help to answer the compelling question. Once the questions are written, sources that might help answer those questions are identified.

2. **Applying disciplinary concepts and tools:** Students use skills and concepts from civics, economics, geography, and history to answer their questions. This dimension focuses on broad skills and concepts so particular content can be decided at the state level.

3. **Evaluating sources and using evidence:** At this stage, students gather sources and evaluate their credibility. Then they identify evidence to answer their questions.

4. **Communicating conclusions and taking informed action:** Finally, students write and critique their arguments built on the evidence. Then based on their conclusions, students plan and implement ways to address the issues explored in the inquiry (NCSS, 2013).

The inquiry design model (IDM) is written to coincide with the C3 framework as a model to support teachers as they design inquiry lessons (Swan et al., 2018). IDM was written to support teachers to put the C3 framework into action and design inquiries for use in their classrooms. The model also includes a design blueprint that supplies teachers with a graphic organizer for their instructional design. The model has three phases: Framing, Filling, and Finishing. The Framing phase includes deciding their "content angle," or how they will approach a given topic from the standards; writing a compelling question to drive the inquiry; and testing out a summative argument task to ensure the question and task align. Then the Filling phase includes writing supporting questions to sustain the inquiry process, locating and considering sources, and building formative performance tasks to help students connect their sources to the compelling question to build their final argument. Finally, the Finishing phase stages the compelling question to build interest and meaning, plans extension activities where students can present their arguments through different media and more audiences, and takes action in the community in connection with the inquiry topic.

The scientific method and other inquiry frameworks exist fundamentally to teach students how to ask and answer questions. While it may not be exactly how scientists, historians, or even detectives try to find information, it prepares students for active citizenship. Each of these models has something to offer teachers and students. But as seen in recent literature, not one approach is universally agreed upon. There is not a single approach that can fit the needs of every inquiry in the classroom and daily life.

Disagreements About Elements of the Inquiry

Currently, the IDM (Swan et al., 2018), based on the NCSS's C3 framework (2013), is a predominant model in K–12 social studies. As mentioned earlier, many lessons seem to loosely use the model, adopting and tweaking some of the elements. Other scholars pose specific critiques or revisions to the IDM based on a specific need.

In a 2018 study, for example, Jacobsen et al. examined how adolescents evaluated sources about school desegregation. They found that the evaluation of evidence varied with emotional or personal and connections to the topic. Their findings and discussion indicate the need of a nuanced approach to source evaluation, and they critique the IDM's neglect of emotion and positionality when evaluating sources

Hlavacik and Krutka (2021) also critique IDM, arguing that its focus on deliberation does not adequately examine issues of injustice. They believe that "civic deliberation and civic litigation can coexist but neither can substitute for the other if a community desires to be both democratic and just," (p. 423). Therefore, there must be a role for litigation in addition to deliberation. Building off of Crowley and King's (2018) recommendations, they propose a model of justice-oriented inquiry, the critical inquiry design model (CIDM), that critiques systems of oppression and includes the voices of marginalized people (p. 421). In CIDM, students focus on the scope of injustice and make accusations and defenses of someone committing injustice instead of pro-and-con arguments about a policy. For example, instead of asking "What is the real cost of bananas?" a CIDM's question might be "Does the banana industry exploit children?" The sources would support students' accusation or defense of the banana industry's actions.

Similarly, Perrotta (2022) also sees potential in the IDM but would revise its focus to promote the development of historical empathy based on Colby's historical narrative inquiry model and the C3 framework with an emphasis on prior knowledge, multiple sources, and the compelling questions (p. 49). As students progress through the inquiry, they are asked about the feelings, perspectives, and insights of those involved in a historical event. To assess the inquiry, she aligned Lee and Shemilt's five-level framework to create a rubric to measure students' historical empathy.

Though several formats have been popular in research and instruction, the disagreements about the elements that "should be" in inquiry persist. This continues to reinforce the idea that there is no one-size-fits-all approach. There is space in the field for several formats and frameworks in order to allow teachers the freedom to develop inquiries that best meet their needs.

Different Types of Inquiry

Regardless of the formats, most social studies inquiries can be classified into three different types: contemporary, historical, and critical. All three will be represented in this book. There is some overlap in these types, as both historical and contemporary can be critical. In addition, a contemporary question may need to include historical background and supporting questions. So while we have divided them into these categories, please note, we consider the categories to be fluid and overarching.

Contemporary

Several of our previously published inquiries would be considered contemporary inquiries (Weber & Hagan, 2020; Hagan & Weber, 2018). They focus on students understanding and addressing contemporary concerns. Contemporary inquiries have compelling questions focusing on an ongoing or current issue. There may be some historical context, but the focus of the compelling question is contemporary. Additional examples of contemporary inquiry are Hong and Melville (2018), Shear et al. (2018), and Weber (2019).

Historical

Historical inquiry focuses on a historical question. Levstik and Barton (2022) wrote about how inquiry can increase students' historical knowledge and allow them to grapple with questions they may already have about history. Historical inquiry allows for the use of primary and secondary sources. Like all inquiries, the compelling question is the center of the inquiry, but the compelling question focuses on a historical topic or event. Additional examples of historical inquiry are Muetterties and Haney (2018), Kucan et al. (2018), and Perrotta (2022).

Critical

The third type of inquiry is critical inquiry. Crowley and King (2018) define critical inquiry as inquiry that "should be designed to identify and to challenge master narratives that legitimate systems of oppression and power" (p. 15). They continue, "Critical inquiries should highlight what these master narratives ignore and provide counter-narratives that complicate and expand students' understanding of the world" (Crowley &

King, 2018, p. 16). Santiago and Dozono (2022) argue that there is a false dichotomy between historical and critical inquiry – that all historical inquiry should be critical. We are leaving them separate here to acknowledge that historical AND contemporary inquiry can (and should) be critical. Examples of critical inquiry are Hughes (2022), Swan et al. (2022), Shear et al. (2018), Kucan et al. (2019), and Muetterties and Haney (2018).

Teachers Need Support

Just as the field has demonstrated a need for versatile approaches to inquiry, research has demonstrated a strong need for teacher training and support in inquiry-based instruction. Many of the teachers in the classroom today have not learned through inquiry and are unfamiliar with the process. Inquiry-based instruction challenges teachers' notions about social studies instruction (Crocco & Marino, 2017, p. 7). Teachers are often familiar with social studies driven by content coverage, memorization, and tests. Inquiry does not fit within this narrow conception of social studies, which is often based in their own educational experiences. Furthermore, there is often little time devoted to elementary social studies instruction, and this time crunch can lead to more teacher-directed inquiry instruction rather than authentic, student-driven inquiry opportunities. Teachers might be hesitant to implement inquiry because they perceive the planning as burdensome (Crocco & Marino, 2017).

Furthermore, the role of teachers is different in inquiry-based learning. Instead of directing the lesson or following a definite plan, teachers must facilitate the process and allow students to take charge of their learning, especially in the older grades. Designing and implementing inquiry requires that teachers have a strong knowledge of the content (Thacker et al., 2018a; McParker, 2021). McParker (2021) explains that social studies is often neglected in the early grades because teachers lack the pedagogical content knowledge. Furthermore, inquiry, using the IDM, requires too high of a level of PCK for many teachers.

But research has also demonstrated that teachers are able to use inquiry in their classes when supported (McParker, 2021; Crocco & Marino, 2017). Through engaging in inquiry during methods classes, both McParker (2021) and Crocco and Marino (2017) saw that pre-service teachers engaged in inquiry. McParker's students were supported to create inquiry units that integrate literacy and social studies. Though pre-service teachers without strong PCK in social studies, his participants designed "high-quality inquiry projects" (p. 18). Crocco and Marino's (2017) participants developed the capacity for inquiry and were motivated to engage in local history inquiries. Both studies uphold the value of engaging in frequent, motivating inquiry experiences in methods classes in order to build teachers' understanding of and motivation for inquiry-based learning. Thacker et al. (2018a) reiterate that in-service teachers also need professional development in order to implement inquiry in their instruction well.

Conclusion

Throughout the literature, inquiry-based instruction is upheld as a powerful learning method. Students have grown in not only content knowledge but also the skills of "doing social studies." Furthermore, the promotion of inquiry by the National Council for Social Studies through the C3 framework (2013), the IDM (Swan et al., 2018), and several states' adoption of inquiry-based standards indicates a strong shift towards inquiry-based social studies. In 2021, 32 state standards either referenced or were modeled upon the C3 framework (New et al., 2021). At the same time, the definition of inquiry is inconsistent in the literature.

Various formats have been discussed and both teacher and student learning have been examined, but it appears that, like in science, a one-size-fits-all approach is not the most practical. Thacker et al. (2018b) found that teachers appreciated the IDM framework because it gave them a structure to work from; however, they used the framework in various ways. It seems to us that the best way to support teachers, then, is not to have a strictly defined format but, rather, to provide a structure that can be easily tweaked to fit their needs.

We conclude that inquiry cannot and should not be taught as a single approach. Just as scientists do not conduct experiments in strict accordance with the scientific method, citizens do not adhere to a specific method of inquiry. At the same time, when beginning inquiries, frameworks can be helpful tools. For this reason, we designed our framework to offer teachers and students another tool that can be modified for the grade level and the comfort level students and teachers have with designing and implementing inquiry. Additionally, it can be modified to give students as much or as little support as they need.

References

Betz, F. (2011). Origin of scientific method. In F. Betz (Ed.), *Managing science: Methodology and organization of research* (pp. 21–41). Springer. https://doi.org/10.1007/978-1-4419-7488-4_2

Bobrowsky, M. (2021, March/April). Q: Do scientists really use the "scientific method?" *Science & Children*, 88–91.

Boyle-Baise, M., & Zevin, J. (2009). *Young citizens of the world*. Routledge.

Brugar, K. A. (2019). Inquiry by the book: Using children's nonfiction as mentor texts for inquiry. *The Social Studies, 110*(4), 155–160. https://doi.org/10.1080/00377996.2019.1581724

Bybee, R. W., & Landes, N. M. (1990). Science for life & living: An elementary school science program from biological sciences curriculum study. *The American Biology Teacher, 52*(2), 92–98. https://doi.org/10.2307/4449042

Casey, E. M., DiCarlo, C. F., & Sheldon, K. L. (2019). Growing democratic citizenship competencies: Fostering social studies understandings through inquiry learning in the preschool garden. *The Journal of Social Studies Research, 43*(4), 361–373. https://doi.org/10.1016/j.jssr.2018.12.001

Crocco, M. S., & Marino, M. P. (2017). Promoting inquiry-oriented teacher preparation in social studies through the use of local history. *The Journal of Social Studies Research, 41*(1), 1–10. https://doi.org/10.1016/j.jssr.2015.11.001

Crowley, R. M., & King, L. J. (2018). Making inquiry critical: Examining power and inequity in the classroom. *Social Education, 82*(1), 14–17.

Cutraro, J. (2012, July 5). Problems with 'the scientific method.' *Science News Explores*. www.snexplores.org/article/problems-scientific-method

Hagan, H. N., & Weber, C. A. (2018). Using inquiry to investigate the global challenge of equal access for girls to an education. *Middle Level Learning, 61*, 1–17.

Hlavacik, M., & Krutka, D. G. (2021). Deliberation can wait" how civic litigation makes inquiry critical. *Theory & Research in Social Education*, 49(3), 418–448. https://doi.org/10.1080/00933104.2021.1933665

Hong, J. E., & Melville, A. (2018). Training social studies teachers to develop inquiry-based GIS lessons. *Journal of Geography*, 117, 229–244. https://doi.org/10.1080/00221341.2017.1371205

Hubbard, K. L., Aker, L. D., & Bentley, J. K. (2021). "We're going to the zoo!" Re-envisioning prop boxes as meaningful and playful inquiry in early childhood social studies. *Social Studies and the Young Learner*, 34(2), 3–9.

Hughes, R. E. (2022). "What is slavery?": Third-grade students' sensemaking about enslavement through historical inquiry. *Theory & Research in Social Education*, 50(1), 29–73. https://doi.org/10.1080/00933104.2021.1927921

Jacobsen, R., Halvorsen, A. L., Frasier, A. S., Schmitt, A., Crocco, M., & Segall, A. (2018). Thinking deeply, thinking emotionally: How high school students make sense of evidence. *Theory & Research in Social Education*, 46(2), 232–276. https://doi.org/10.1080/00933104.2018.1425170

Kim, E. J., & Falkner, A. (2022). "Not your model minority": An inquiry on the immigration and nationality act of 1965. *Social Studies and the Young Learner*, 34(3), 14–18.

Kucan, L., Rainey, E., & Cho, B. Y. (2019). Engaging middle school students in disciplinary literacy through culturally relevant historical inquiry. *Journal of Adolescent & Adult Literacy*, 63(1), 15–27. https://doi.org/10.1002/jaal.940

Levstik, L. S., & Barton, K. C. (2022). *Doing history: Investigating with children in elementary and middle school*. Routledge. https://doi.org/10.4324/9781003179658

McNeill, K. L., & Martin, D. M. (2011). Claims, evidence, and reasoning: Demystifying data during a unit on simple machines. *Science & Children*, 48(8), 52.

McParker, M. C. (2021). Where are we? A process for developing elementary inquiries. *Social Studies and the Young Learner*, 34(2), 14–18.

Mehta, M. P. (2022). Using digital archives to teach early South Asian American histories. *Social Studies and the Young Learner*, 34(3), 19–24.

Muetterties, C., & Haney, J. (2018). How did slavery shape my state? Using inquiry to explore Kentucky history. *Social Studies and the Young Learner*, 30(3), 20–25.

Muetterties, C., Slocum, C., & Masterson, E. (2020). What is a vote worth? A focused inquiry to scaffold elementary historical thinking. *The Social Studies, 111*(3), 133–142. https://doi.org/10.1080/00377996.2019.1706070

National Council for the Social Studies. (2013). *Social studies for the next generation: Purposes, practices, and implications of the college, career, and civic life (C3) framework for social studies state standard.* NCSS Publications. www.socialstudies.org/sites/default/files/c3/c3-framework-for-social-studies-rev0617.pdf

New, R., Swan, K., Lee, J., & Grant, S. G. (2021). The state of social studies standards: What is the impact of the C3 framework? *Social Education, 85*(4), 239–246.

Payne, K. A., & Green, E. (2018). Inquiry through the lens of identity: An exploration and inquiry in the fifth grade. *Social Studies and the Young Learner, 30*(3), 4–8.

Perrotta, K. (2022). Using historical empathy strategies to analyze Elizabeth Jennings v. The Third Avenue Railway Company. *Social Education, 86*(1), 47–56.

Santiago, M., & Dozono, T. (2022). History is critical: Addressing the false dichotomy between historical inquiry and criticality. *Theory & Research in Social Education,* 1–23. https://doi.org/10.1080/00933104.2022.2048426

Shear, S. B., Sabzalian, L., & Buchanan, L. B. (2018). Affirming Indigenous sovereignty: A civics inquiry. *Social Studies and the Young Learner, 31*(1), 12–18.

Swan, K., Crowley, R., Stamoulacatos, N., Lewis, B., & Stringer, G. (2022). Countering the past of least resistance: A hard history inquiry-based curriculum. *Social Education, 86*(1), 34–39.

Swan, K., Lee, J., & Grant, S. G. (2018). *Inquiry design model: Building inquiries in social studies.* National Council for the Social Studies.

Thacker, E. S., Friedman, A. M., Fitchett, P. G., Journell, W., & Lee, J. K. (2018a). Exploring how an elementary teacher plans and implements social studies inquiry. *The Social Studies, 109*(2), 85–100. https://doi.org/10.1080/00377996.2018.1451983

Thacker, E. S., Lee, J. K., Fitchett, P. G., & Journell, W. (2018b). Secondary social studies teachers' experiences planning and implementing inquiry using the inquiry design model. *The Clearing House, 91*(4–5), 193–200. https://doi.org/10.1080/00098655.2018.1490129

Wargo, J. M., & Alvarado, J. (2020). "Making" civics and designing inquiry: Integrative, project-based learning in pre-kindergarten. *Social Studies and the Young Learner, 33*(1), 28–32.

Weber, C. A. (2019). Teaching about sprots icons and gender equity. *Middle Level Learning, 66,* 1–12.

Weber, C. A., & Hagan, H. N. (2020). Is the right to clean water fake news? An elementary inquiry lesson exploring media literacy and human rights. *Social Studies and the Young Learner, 33*(1), 3–9.

3

HOW SHOULD WE APPROACH INQUIRY IN THE CLASSROOM?

With the publication of the C3 framework (NCSS, 2013) and its emphasis on inquiry-based social studies came a rise in states rewriting social studies standards to reflect inquiry (Cuenca, 2021). Chiefly, the C3 framework has been widely used and is the basis for several journal articles (Brugar, 2019; Crocco & Marino, 2017; Hong & Melville, 2018). While we have referenced the C3 in previous articles (Hagan & Weber, 2018; Weber, 2019; Weber & Hagan, 2020), we always found that it didn't quite meet our needs or the needs of our pre-service teachers. We wanted an inquiry model that is adaptable to student needs and development and, eventually, teaches students how to create their own inquiries. Furthermore, we wanted reflection to be an integral part of inquiry. One of our main components involves students writing and revising a hypothesis to answer the compelling question. We feel that the hypothesis is an important part of learning through inquiry and provides teaching opportunities. In this chapter, we provide an overview of

DOI: 10.4324/9781003274148-4

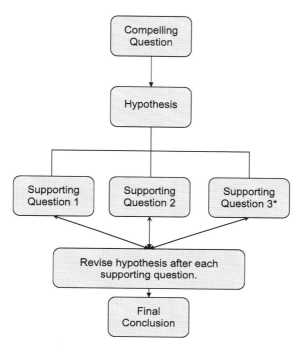

Figure 3.1 Our inquiry framework

Note: This framework can be used for more than three supporting questions.

the framework and how it can be adapted for different grade levels and differentiated for different abilities.

Framework Overview

Our framework consists of several components, which work together to create an inquiry. The components include the compelling question, hypothesis, supporting questions (including opportunities to revise the hypothesis after each supporting question), and a final conclusion. Each section is important to scaffold students as the teacher facilitates their thinking and exploration.

The inquiry process begins with, and is guided by, the compelling question. While compelling questions and essential questions can be similar and are often used interchangeably, we prefer compelling questions. Essential questions, as explained by Wiggins and McTighe (2005), are "provocative, arguable, and likely to generate inquiry around the central ideas" (p. 28). Whereas compelling questions "focus on enduring issues and concerns. They deal with curiosities about how things work; interpretations and applications of disciplinary concepts; and unresolved issues that require students to construct arguments in response" (NCSS (C3), 2013, p. 23). While they are very similar, we prefer the term compelling, as it has the connotation of evoking interest, whereas essential focuses on what is necessary or required. Compelling questions also can, and should, be multidisciplinary, an important aspect of the multidisciplinary subject of social studies.

An entire inquiry is aimed at answering the compelling question. When using this framework, there are two possible directions: teacher-driven or student-driven. We recommend that the first few inquiries have a teacher-driven compelling question. Once students have learned the inquiry process, teachers may begin to release part (or, eventually, all) of the planning to students. This may begin with the teacher allowing students to choose a topic and then guiding the students to write a compelling question together as a class. It also could lead to students asking their own questions or choosing a topic of interest to them.

To introduce the topic, we recommend short videos, read-alouds, or pictures to tap into students' prior knowledge. Activating students' prior knowledge and/or introducing the topic allows for students to become engaged in the topic or to see why the compelling question is being asked. Additionally, activating prior knowledge can help them write a hypothesis that better reflects their current understanding and make connections with their new learning. The introduction might also be used to introduce a new concept or present a bit of background knowledge but is not the place for extensive lessons. For example, in the inquiry about global issues (see Chapter 10), students begin the class with viewing a photo essay and infographics from UNICEF, allowing them to get the larger picture of the UN Universal Declaration of Human Rights before delving specifically into girls' education. The pictures capture student interest and, along with the infographics, introduce students to the UN Declaration of Human Rights. We prefer a brief introduction to generate student interest. If the inquiry is student-driven, small groups of students may provide the introduction to their classmates.

After the introduction and listening to the compelling question again, learners consider their background and experiences to write a hypothesis. The hypothesis is the first step in answering the compelling question and allows students to think through their ideas and begin to work on "putting it all together." As Dewey says, "We do not learn from experience. We learn from reflection on experience. Reliving an experience leads to making connections between information and feelings produced by the experience" (Dewey, 1933, p. 78). While writing a hypothesis for inquiry outside of science is not new (see Dewey, 1933; Parker, 2005; Boyle-Baise & Zevin, 2009, 2014), it is not included in the C3 framework. This notion of the importance of reflection in learning is one of the primary and important components of our framework. Our model requires students to reflect on their prior experiences and knowledge to hypothesize about the compelling question before reviewing any sources or engaging in any activity. Not only does this reflection trigger background knowledge, but it can help teachers identify misconceptions immediately, thus serving as an ongoing formative assessment during the inquiry. As the facilitator, they can then support learning by guiding students in a way that pushes them to confront those misconceptions. This is another opportunity to allow for students to take on more of the responsibility by guiding them to reliable sources from multiple perspectives to challenge misconceptions. Furthermore, our framework asks students to revisit their hypothesis as they answer each supporting question. Again, this requires students to reflect on their new findings at each step along the way. It requires them to continue to revisit their prior knowledge and previous thinking in order to refine and revise it to accommodate their new learning. We believe there is value in this process. Not only does it prompt them to reflect on their prior thinking but it also allows them to understand their thought process, serving as a sort of map for how their conclusion developed.

Additionally, revising their hypothesis regularly allows students to revise and refine their writing about social studies. Even though writing is frequently part of social studies, the ability to revise their writing about social studies is often absent (Bickford et al., 2020). Students are frequently instructed to complete research and write an essay without the opportunity to refine or revise their thinking. Framing the inquiry in a way which allows for students to revise their ideas when presented with new information models how to write about social studies.

After writing a hypothesis, learners consider one or more supporting questions. Each of the supporting questions acts as a stepping stone towards answering the compelling question. Usually, in our inquiries, the supporting questions are designed as stations, where students explore resources independently or in small groups. These can also be completed as a whole class, one at a time. For early inquiries, we recommend creating graphic organizers to help students analyze the new information at each station (these are provided for the lessons in Part 2). As students take part in more inquiries and are taught how to evaluate sources, they can begin to choose the sources and even write the supporting questions. While our graphic in the previous section shows three supporting questions, there can be more if that fits the inquiry. For example, the inquiry in Chapter 10 about global issues includes seven different supporting questions.

After answering each supporting question, the learner returns to the hypothesis and makes revisions based on what they just learned. Then they move on to the next supporting question. Each time a student revises their hypothesis is an opportunity for a formative assessment. Teachers can use this opportunity to check for misconceptions. If students have misconceptions, teachers can address them before students go to the next station or they can challenge students to recognize possible misconceptions.

Once all the supporting questions have been answered and the hypothesis has been revised a final time, the learner synthesizes their work into their final conclusion. They are encouraged to use all the information from the supporting questions to support their thinking. The final conclusion is an opportunity for students to share their responses to the compelling question. They can also reflect on how their thinking has changed from their original hypothesis. As students begin to design their own inquiries, they need to focus on learning opportunities and how to answer their own compelling and supporting questions. Finally, the conclusion is also a chance for students to discuss if any next steps or actions are necessary. This part should always be student-driven and focused on their interests and/or identified needs.

Our framework relies heavily on reflective thinking. Students reflect on the compelling question after any new information. They refine and revise their thinking throughout. Finally, they construct a conclusion based on evidence from reliable sources. This emphasis not only aids their learning about the concept but also about the inquiry process. As they see their thinking change according to their new findings, they better understand how each piece of information increases their understanding. Furthermore, continuing to refine and revise the hypothesis helps as they develop flexible thinking.

Adaptability

This framework consists of the basic components of compelling question, hypothesis, supporting questions, and final conclusion. Thacker et al. (2018) noted that even with a well-developed framework, teachers often make tweaks to best fit their needs. Therefore, we have made our framework easily adaptable and described possible adaptations with each lesson. Ideally, teachers would be able to gradually withdraw support so students can become more independent as they use this framework to engage in inquiry. Eventually, the process will become more student-led, with them asking their own questions, identifying sources, and engaging with much of the process independently. It is important that the teacher continues to facilitate but that students take the lead. Some of the provided adaptations provide ways teachers can provide more support or increase student independence. The framework is also easily adaptable to multiple topics by changing the question; writing more or fewer supporting questions; or using a variety of sources including primary sources, charts, maps, articles, or documentaries (see Chapter 4 for more ideas of where to find sources for the supporting questions). In the next section, we go through how inquiry can be scaffolded for early childhood, intermediate grades, and middle level.

Early Childhood

The National Association for the Education of Young Children (NAEYC) (2020) names several developmentally appropriate practices for early childhood education. We believe this inquiry framework touches specifically on three of them. First, children are organizing and creating meaning through their experiences. Second, children want to learn when school learning is connected to what they learn at home and in their community. Third, content integration is key to student learning. This framework allows for students to create meaning through their reflections on answering the compelling question. They look at sources to organize and create. Inquiry allows students to use their background knowledge from their home and community lives to answer questions at school. Third, this inquiry framework works best when multidisciplinary.

The focus, in the beginning for this age, should be how to do inquiry – that means teachers will pose the compelling question and supporting questions. For the most part, the teacher will also find the sources and guide students to the final conclusion. However, as students learn the process, there is no reason they cannot begin to formulate compelling and supporting questions with the teacher's guidance. Maybe the children express interest in a topic and the teacher helps them to refine the questions and find sources. Sometimes the best sources at this grade are pictures, videos, artifacts, or items that the teacher can read aloud to the students. Source evaluation can also be introduced at this age, albeit very simply. With support, students can discuss why one source might be better than another because it is relevant to the question. They can also examine if a source contains facts or opinions.

Intermediate Grades

In the intermediate grades, students should be able to create compelling and, with scaffolding, supporting questions. At this age, teachers will likely need to act as facilitators to help students refine questions and find sources. The teacher may need to still provide sources, though students might be able to locate their own with support or select the most appropriate sources from a list. Sources can continue to be pictures, videos, or artifacts, but books, websites, and infographics can also be introduced. This is an ideal time to start scaffolding how to evaluate sources (see Chapter 9). Then teachers can model how to determine the reliability of sources. As intermediate students continue to complete inquiries, they will begin to be able to evaluate sources to use. Teachers can still use the hypothesis to formatively assess students throughout the inquiry.

Middle School

By the time students reach middle school, they should be designing most of the inquiries themselves, especially if they have participated in inquiry lessons throughout elementary school. Inquiry can be a powerful learning tool in the middle grades. Bishop and Harrison (2021), in the Association for Middle Level Education's updated position paper, call for curriculum that is "challenging, exploratory, integrative, and diverse" (p. 27) and instruction that "fosters learning that is active, purposeful, and democratic" (p. 35). Inquiry, using this framework, can be all of these things.

While middle school students will not require the same scaffolding as early childhood or intermediate students, they will require scaffolding to help them develop as critical thinkers. They may choose a topic but then need assistance writing compelling and supporting questions that dig deeper into the topics. They may be able to find sources but may need help, at first, evaluating their accuracy.

Additionally, inquiry in the middle grades can involve partnering with other content area teachers. Unlike in elementary school, where one teacher can combine reading and social studies (or other content areas), in middle school, this may require collaboration between various content area teachers. Inquiries can be part of a team-wide lesson or unit.

If middle school students have not spent their elementary school years learning how to do inquiries and scaffolding to take control of the process, they will need more guidance than if they had these experiences. They may need to complete one or two teacher-designed inquiries to learn the process. Then teachers can scaffold so that students start to choose topics, and the teacher helps them to write compelling and supporting questions. Or maybe the teacher begins by giving the students the questions but helps students learn to find and evaluate sources to answer the questions. The important thing is to gradually teach students how to do each aspect of the inquiry framework until they begin to ask their own questions, find their own (reliable) sources, and draw final conclusions.

Finally, we also highly recommend partnering with the school librarian to help find and evaluate sources, no matter the age of the students. In early childhood, intermediate, or middle-level classrooms, the school librarian can be a valuable resource.

Differentiation

Differentiation is also possible with the framework. Some lessons may include different source material for different students. Other lessons may be completed in small groups, where each group works on a different supporting question before reporting back to the class and working together to formulate a conclusion. Technology can be included to allow materials to be read to students or translated into their native language. Throughout the lessons provided in Chapter 2, there are ideas for specific differentiation strategies.

Types of Inquiry

Several researchers who justify the use of inquiry in social studies (Barton & Levstik, 2004; Thornton, 2001) mostly discuss historical inquiry. While the inquiry process described in this book can be used for students to grapple with historical questions, it can also be used for students to explore contemporary questions. As described in Chapter 2, both historical and contemporary inquiries can be critical as well. While historical and contemporary are represented in this book, this framework also works well for critical inquiry. The hypothesis, especially, allows teachers to frequently check for misconceptions. The introductory portion of the lesson followed by the first hypothesis helps teachers know how much of the master narrative students have heard or believe. Then supporting questions and sources can be used to introduce counter-narratives. Again, teachers should then use the reflection of the hypothesis after each supporting question to continuously check for misconceptions and support students as their thinking evolves.

Conclusion

Our framework consists of four main parts: compelling question, hypothesis, supporting questions, and final conclusions. Unlike some of the other frameworks, ours emphasizes the hypothesis and reflective thought. Importantly, the steps of writing and revising the hypothesis allow teachers to identify and address misconceptions along the way. Also, students can see how their thinking changes with each new piece of information. They can learn how to adapt their understanding to incorporate new knowledge.

Furthermore, we have designed this framework to be versatile. It can be used for any grade level and with any type of inquiry. It also can be scaffolded to teach students to develop their own questions and find their own sources. This versatility allows teachers the chance to use, design, and implement inquiry-based lessons and units in the way that best fits the needs of their class and content.

References

Barton, K. C., & Levstik, L. S. (2004). *Teaching history for the common good*. Routledge.

Bickford, J. H., Clabough, J., & Taylor, T. (2020). Fourth graders'(re-) reading, (historical) thinking, and (revised) writing about the black freedom movement. *The Journal of Social Studies Research*, 44(2), 249–261. https://doi.org/10.1016/j.jssr.2020.01.001

Bishop, P. A., & Harrison, L. M. (2021). *The successful middle school: This we believe*. Association for Middle Level Education.

Boyle-Baise, M., & Zevin, J. (2009). *Young citizens of the world: Teaching elementary social studies through civic engagement*. Routledge.

Boyle-Baise, M., & Zevin, J. (2014). *Young citizens of the world: Teaching elementary social studies through civic engagement* (2nd ed.). Routledge.

Brugar, K. A. (2019). Inquiry by the book: Using children's nonfiction as mentor texts for inquiry. *The Social Studies*, 110(4), 155–160. https://doi.org/10.1080/00377996.2019.1581724

Crocco, M. S., & Marino, M. P. (2017). Promoting inquiry-oriented teacher preparation in social studies through the use of local history. *The Journal of Social Studies Research*, 41(1), 1–10. https://doi.org/10.1016/j.jssr.2015.11.001

Cuenca, A. (2021). Proposing core practices for social studies teacher education: A qualitative content analysis of inquiry-based lessons.

Journal of Teacher Education, 72(3), 298–313. https://doi.org/10.1177/00224871209480

Dewey, J. (1933). *How we think: A restatement of the relation of reflective thinking to the educative process.* D.C. Heath and Company. http://books.google.com/books?id=WF0AAAAAMAAJ&printsec=frontcover&dq=john+dewey&hl=en&ei=3NnFTJPvHdOInQee1_XVCQ&sa=X&oi=book_result&ct=book-preview-link&resnum=3&ved=0CEIQuwUwAg#v=onepage&q&f=false

Hagan, H. N., & Weber, C. A. (2018). Using inquiry to investigate the global challenge of equal access for girls to an education. *Middle Level Learning, 61,* 1–17.

Hong, J. E., & Melville, A. (2018). Training social studies teachers to develop inquiry-based GIS lessons. *Journal of Geography, 117,* 229–244. https://doi.org/10.1080/00221341.2017.1371205

NAEYC. (2020). *Developmentally appropriate practice* [Position statement]. NAEYC. www.naeyc.org/resources/position-statements/dap/principles

National Council for the Social Studies. (2013). *The college, career, and civic life (C3) framework for social studies state standards: Guidance for enhancing the rigor of K-12 civics, economics, geography, and history.* National Council for the Social Studies.

Parker, W. (2005). *Social studies in elementary education* (12th ed.). Pearson Merrill/Prentice Hall.

Thacker, E. S., Lee, J. K., Fitchett, P. G., & Journell, W. (2018). Secondary social studies teachers' experiences planning and implementing inquiry using the inquiry design model. *The Clearing House, 91*(4–5), 193–200.

Thornton, S. J. (2001). Legitimacy in the social studies curriculum. In L. Corno (Ed.), *Education across a century: The centennial volume. One hundredth yearbook of the national society for the study of education, part 1.* The University of Chicago Press.

Weber, C. A. (2019). Teaching about sports icons and gender equity. *Middle Level Learning, 66,* 1–12.

Weber, C. A., & Hagan, H. N. (2020). Is the right to clean water fake news? An elementary inquiry lesson exploring media literacy and human rights. *Social Studies and the Young Learner, 33*(1), 3–9.

Wiggins, G. P., & McTighe, J. (2005). *Understanding by design.* ASCD.

4

PEDAGOGICAL CONTENT KNOWLEDGE

Content for Teachers and Students

"Teachers can't teach what they don't know" is a common statement within teacher education. But it leaves out the nuances between content and pedagogy and how teachers need to be prepared for both. In order to teach with inquiry, teachers need to know the content they are introducing to students, the pedagogy of inquiry, and the pedagogical content knowledge related to both inquiry and the specific topic they are teaching to that particular group of students. Teachers must have a working knowledge that goes well beyond the given standards.

When we plan our units, we focus on pedagogy, content, and how to combine those into pedagogical content knowledge. Because Chapter 3 focused almost completely on pedagogy, specifically the inquiry framework that is the basis for this book, this chapter will focus on how teachers can better understand the content of the inquiry lessons they design. Of course, the content of inquiry lessons can vary widely, so we will focus on how and where to locate sources both for teachers and students

DOI: 10.4324/9781003274148-5

by providing some general strategies as well as our "go-to" sources when we are preparing to teach a new topic.

Content

Teacher Background Knowledge

When we begin to plan inquiry lessons, our first step is always to research the topic of the inquiry. Social studies spans a great amount of knowledge, which is constantly evolving. Even the most experienced educators and experts must continuously develop their content knowledge. Once we have a basic idea of the topic, we can find sources that are appropriate for our students. Without this first dive into teacher resources, we would struggle with how to locate the most appropriate sources for students or how help them find and evaluate their own sources. Teachers need strong background knowledge, but it is impractical to read lengthy books or attend professional development on everything in our standards.

The lessons we have published and our conference presentations always come with a resource sheet (Hagan & Weber, 2018; Weber & Hagan, 2020). If we are creating a historical inquiry, we look at historical societies, archives, or museum websites. If we are planning more contemporary inquiries, we often look at nonprofit or governmental organizations and media websites appropriate to our topic, such as the UN or newspapers. When designing your own inquiries, background knowledge is just as important. As you plan your instruction, we encourage you to annotate the resources you use, as they might be helpful to you in the future or to those with whom you share your lessons. Also, pay attention to sources that are appropriate for student use or should only be used for teachers.

The remainder of this section is dedicated to some of the teacher resources we have found to be commonly helpful. Although these resources are not specific to every topic you may teach, our goal is to equip teachers with a few trusted resources that cover background information for a multitude of possible topics.

Professional Organizations Offering Teacher Resources and Professional Development

Please note:

The dynamic nature of the internet makes it difficult to direct teachers to helpful websites. Therefore, our suggestions will focus on organizations, rather than websites. However, each organization has a website with very supportive teacher resources. A simple search of the name should connect you with up-to-date website addresses.

Colleagues

Teaching is seldom a solo journey. We usually teach in teams according to grade level or subject matter. This presents the opportunity to learn from each other. Perhaps a colleague is fascinated with the Civil War and can share some information and resources with you. Some teams ask teachers to develop expertise in one of the areas they will teach that year and present it to their teammates. Once each member has focused and presented on one area, the entire team has developed some knowledge and been given resources so they are equipped to teach that topic.

Council for Economic Education

The Council for Economic Education offers classroom resources for teachers of all grade levels. These resources focus on personal finance and economic principles. In-person and online, free professional development is also available through their teacher-focused site, EconEdLink.

Historical Societies

If you are looking at local history, checking the local historical society for information is a great place to start. Oftentimes, local resources will not be available online or may be difficult to locate. Historical societies are wonderful places to find primary sources, and there are frequent volunteers who have a wealth of local knowledge.

Library of Congress

The Library of Congress has primary sources available as well as professional development. It offers professional development and resources for how to analyze primary sources and offers a service where you can chat with a librarian. Particularly useful is the classroom materials section, which includes primary source sets, presentations, and lesson plans about a wide range of topics. The primary source analysis tool is helpful for both teachers and students, as it walks you through the process of analyzing different types of sources.

Local Libraries

Libraries often subscribe to databases, allowing you to find information for free that you might not have access to otherwise. Furthermore, librarians are helpful in finding information for both adults and children, particularly about local historical and contemporary topics. Additionally, librarians can help find children's literature for text sets matching your topic.

National Archives

The National Archives has a wealth of primary sources that teachers can analyze to build background knowledge. However, they also have webinars and other professional development to support teachers in using those resources and learning how to analyze primary sources. The educator section provides primary source analysis worksheets that are available in English and Spanish for a variety of grade levels. Additionally, the DocsTeach area can be particularly helpful because it provides groups of primary sources according to the topic as well as activities and instructional design tools.

National Council for the Social Studies and State Social Studies Councils

The National Council for the Social Studies (NCSS) is the national organization dedicated to social studies education across settings and disciplines. NCSS published the National Curriculum Standards for Social Studies as well as the college, career, and civic life (C3) framework for Social Studies State Standards. The organization hosts professional learning opportunities virtually and face to face. NCSS also publishes journals for several educational levels and contexts as well as an annual list of notable trade books. Many of these publications are available for free on their website. Furthermore, many states have their own affiliated organizations that provide resources and professional development that support that state's standards and history.

National Geographic

National Geographic has several types of resources teachers might find helpful, such as databases of maps, media, and lesson plans that connect to various topics across disciplines and subject areas. The organization's resources are founded upon the framework of supporting learners as they develop the attitudes, skills, and knowledge of explorers. Similar to NCSS, National Geographic has affiliated state organizations that provide resources and professional development that support that state's standards and geography.

National Parks and National Historical Sites

The National Park Service website is searchable by topic, park, or national site. The educators' areas provide lesson plans, digital collections, professional development, and even travelling resources, which can be delivered to your classroom. Furthermore, national historical sites will have primary sources and secondary sources on their websites and frequently have virtual tours.

University Faculty and Work

If there is a university in your area, there is likely an expert who can support your understanding by discussing a topic with you or offering resources. Sometimes these experts may welcome the opportunity to share with your class or to engage them in experiential learning in their field. Oftentimes, if the faculty member you contact is unable to help you, they may connect you with graduate students or other faculty who have knowledge of the topic.

Content for Students

Pedagogical content knowledge also focuses on determining the most important information and finding appropriate sources to teach students in a particular context. As students develop their understanding of the inquiry process, we gradually teach them how to find and evaluate sources themselves. When they can identify and evaluate sources, they have more independence and control over their inquiries.

Burstein and Hutton (2005) write about how students, even as young as fourth grade, realize that the textbook does not always tell the whole story. The students in this fourth-grade class questioned the textbook's portrayal of Japanese internment and so the teacher was able to find multiple sources, which taught different perspectives (including those from people who lived in the internment camps). While Burstein and Hutton (2005) did not use inquiry to supplement the textbook, their article points to the need for teachers to not completely rely on textbooks in social studies. One benefit of teaching with inquiry is that students can use sources besides textbooks. When planning inquiry, sources vary by the age and level of the students. For example, if one were to teach about elections through inquiry, the sources would look very different between a kindergarten classroom and a sixth-grade classroom. A kindergarten classroom might use election posters, buttons, or videos as sources. A sixth-grade classroom might also use these but, additionally, look at transcripts of a speech or analyze a political commercial for more depth. Using a variety of sources is also a good differentiation strategy. Students can analyze sources in groups or independently to support their thinking in different ways. Additionally, photographs, artifacts, or artwork might be used for struggling readers or students who speak English as a second language. Having access to a variety of sources allows teachers to use their knowledge of the students' strengths and interests to find materials that will best fit the student and classroom needs.

There are many different types of sources, but we will focus primarily on four different types that teachers and students might use and can often be accessed digitally: primary sources, artifacts, children's literature, and online resources.

Primary Sources

Primary sources provide direct reporting of a historical event. They are written or created at the time being studied and are the sources used by historians. In inquiry, they can both inspire more questions and provide evidence for conclusions (Barton & Levstik, 2004, p. 202). At first glance, they might seem like a perfect fit for classroom inquiry; however, it is important to note that students must be scaffolded to engage in primary source analysis. Teachers must be sure that students have enough background knowledge to analyze the source (McCormick, 2004). They should also determine when supporting students through typed transcripts or versions with simplified language is appropriate. Furthermore, primary source analysis guides and worksheets can be helpful to guide the process of working with primary sources. These resources ask important questions and focus the reader on key aspects of the source that might be missed otherwise. We frequently use the worksheets available on the National Archives website in our own classrooms (see Chapter 8 for more information and a lesson plan using primary sources).

At the same time, students (and teachers) should not make the assumption that primary sources are 100% accurate. Students still need to evaluate these sources for biases and misinformation. In his book, Bruce VanSledright (2002) wrote about teaching with primary sources in a fifth-grade classroom. Students investigated primary sources with differing biases and reports, such as a primary source account of the Battle of Lexington from the Colonist perspective and one from the perspective of a British soldier. Both the Colonial Soldiers and the British Soldiers had participated in the battle. The students grappled with how to make sense of primary sources with different biases and sides of a historical event.

Artifacts

Second, while a form of primary sources, artifacts deserve a section all on their own. Artifacts are tactile evidence that students can see and touch. They can be difficult to find, but local historical societies or museums can be helpful. Sometimes, you can also borrow artifacts from museums or national historic sites. Usually, these are loaned to teachers for free, but shipping costs might be required. Teachers can also locate their own replicas. For example, Macken (2008) wrote in *Social Studies and the Young Learner* about using artifacts from the era of Grover Cleveland to teach about the duties of the president. Although her local museum had traveling resources available, she wanted to use them for a lengthier unit. She secured a grant from an antique society and purchased her own artifacts from antique stores in her area. That also gave students the freedom to use these artifacts in their own presentations, and her first graders were very motivated to show off their new learning.

Children's Literature

Children's literature is another important area to be used as evidence in inquiry lessons. It is important, though, to select books carefully and to use children's literature that is accurate, accessible, and appropriate. For example, *The Little House on the Prairie* books are often used to teach about Westward Expansion; however, Wilder's treatment of Native Americans is offensive. Several awards such as the NCSS's Carter G. Woodson Award, NCSS's Notable Trade Books List, and the Coretta Scott King Book Award signal strong children's literature that appropriately represents all cultures. If you are studying a particular culture, there are specific lists or resources to aid selection. For example, a good resource to use to evaluate texts about Indigenous people is Debbie Reese's blog: https:// americanindiansinchildrensliterature.blogspot.com/ (see Chapter 6 for more information and a lesson plan using children's literature).

Online Resources

Primary sources, artifacts, and children's literature can be found online, but there are many more things that students can use when given an opportunity to search for evidence, especially when the inquiry question focuses on contemporary issues. For example, in Chapter 10, we use information from the websites of several nonprofit organizations, newspapers, and United Nations' committees to explore issues in girls' education. Keep in mind that it is important to carefully select sources that are being used in the classroom, especially those from the internet (see Chapter 9 for more information and a lesson plan about evaluating sources).

Scaffolding Students for Independence

Ultimately, the goal of inquiry instruction is for students to develop the skills to build their background knowledge, create compelling questions, identify sources, and evaluate a source's reliability independently. The development of those skills occurs with strategic instruction and withdrawing scaffolding over time. In the early grades, we suggest that students and teachers work together to construct questions. From there, teachers can model how they selected sources and the ways they know it is reliable. Eventually, teachers can pick a few sources and ask students to choose the ones they find to be appropriate for answering their questions. When students make their selections, it will be important for them to support their selection with evidence about the source's reliability. During this time, teachers can show students ways to locate sources and model the process. Teachers can also enlist librarians and media specialists to work with students to develop information literacy and search skills for a variety of media. Middle school students should be able to locate many of their sources, though they will still need support in finding primary sources and evaluating the sources they select.

Conclusion

Content knowledge, the second component of PCK, is unique in that both teachers and students must develop it. This chapter provided several places where teachers could develop their own content knowledge at a deeper level than what is being taught in the classroom. Furthermore, teachers must also select the most appropriate content for students to learn and support students' development of the skills to locate and evaluate their own information – how to develop their own content knowledge to support their thinking and inquiry. We also provided several sources to facilitate the development of student content knowledge.

References

Barton, K. C., & Levstik, L. S. (2004). *Teaching history for the common good.* Routledge.

Burstein, J. H., & Hutton, L. (2005). Planning and teaching with multiple perspectives. *Social Studies and the Young Learner, 18*(1), 15–17.

Hagan, H. N., & Weber, C. A. (2018). The global challenge of equal access for girls to an education: An investigation using inquiry. *Middle Level Learning, 61.*

Macken, C. (2008). Artifacts bring Grover Cleveland's presidency to life in the first grade. *Social Studies and the Young Learner, 21*(2), 8–10.

McCormick, T. M. (2004). Letters from Trenton, 1776: Teaching with primary sources. *Social Studies and the Young Learner, 17*(2), 5–12.

VanSledright, B. (2002). *In search of America's past: Learning to read history in elementary school.* Teachers College Press.

Weber, C. A., & Hagan, H. N. (2020). Is the "right to clean water" fake news? An inquiry in media literacy and human rights. *Social Studies and the Young Learner, 33*(1).

PART II

TEACHING WITH INQUIRY

Now that we have established why teachers should teach with inquiry and given an overview of how to teach with inquiry, Part 2 will explore the process of using inquiry in the classroom with each chapter delving into a particular approach of inquiry-based instruction: using technology, integrating literature, utilizing civic agency, using primary sources, evaluating sources, and focusing on global issues. We will continue to use the framework of pedagogical content knowledge for each chapter, describing the content knowledge for the approach and then presenting the pedagogy of teaching it in the classroom, including a lesson plan.

Each chapter will be formatted in this way:

1. **Introduction to Approach:** The secret to any good instruction is teachers' expertise in blending the pedagogy and content to fit their classes' needs. Therefore, the beginning of each chapter seeks to support teachers in better understanding that chapter's approach in order to make it their own.

DOI: 10.4324/9781003274148-6

2. **Content Knowledge for the Topic:** This section provides resources for teachers to build their own background knowledge about the content covered in that chapter's lesson. Some lessons may offer student resources too. Many of the resources will pertain directly to the topic at hand. However, in some chapters, there are resources related to the topic more generally. For example, in Chapter 5, the lesson concerns the right to education but the content resources look at human rights and the rights of children as a whole.

3. **Pedagogical Knowledge for the Approach:** This section presents the inquiry plan.

   a. *Lesson Plan and Resources:* The lesson plan section activates background knowledge, introduces the compelling question, and elicits a hypothesis. Then the procedures for the inquiry process are laid out, where students gather evidence from multiple sources to answer the supporting questions and revise their hypothesis accordingly. Finally, students synthesize their findings into a conclusion, and in some lessons, ideas for possible extensions are provided.

   b. *Adaptability and Differentiation:* Following each lesson plan, there are some ideas for adapting and differentiating the lesson plan to multiple contexts and student needs. In each chapter, we outline ways to adapt it to early childhood and/or middle-level classrooms. We also offer some ways to accommodate special needs. These sections are in no way exhaustive, but we hope that they are helpful in planning for your particular students.

We have chosen to highlight six different approaches or contexts for teaching with inquiry:

Chapter 5: Using Technology
Chapter 6: Integrating Literature
Chapter 7: Utilizing Civic Agency
Chapter 8: Using Primary Sources
Chapter 9: Evaluating Sources
Chapter 10: Focusing on Global Issues

We made a conscious choice to avoid dividing these lessons by subject/ content areas and by grade level. We avoided subject/content areas, such as history, economics, or geography, in order to honor the interdisciplinary nature of social studies. Social studies was designed to bring these different subjects together and we wanted to make sure our lessons reflected that. Second, we did not create separate lessons for early childhood, intermediate grades, or middle level based on the approach because we believe these approaches can be used for all grade levels. Instead, we include adaptations for each lesson to make it suitable for early childhood or middle level.

Finally, we chose these topics because they provide a good overview of the different ways this framework can be used. It is clearly not an exhaustive list but can provide a starting point for teachers who are learning how to integrate inquiry into their social studies classrooms. At the end of each chapter, we provide a graphic organizer that students can use to keep track of their hypothesis revisions and final conclusions.

Part 2 is where the pedagogy and content merge for the delivery of instruction. We trust that teachers are experts of their own standards, classrooms, and students. It is our hope that the following chapters empower teachers to use the lesson plans to teach through inquiry but also allow plenty of adaptability for educators to employ their professional expertise to make the lessons best suit their needs.

5

USING TECHNOLOGY

Introduction to Approach

Since the COVID pandemic began, teachers have become more familiar with available technologies and have continued some new practices after returning to their classrooms. Our society is now more familiar with online collaboration, instruction, and interactive virtual tools. However, as teachers use technology in their instruction, it is important that it is used purposefully. It may be easy to continue new practices because students enjoy them or because they make grading easier, but it is crucial that the practices we adopt maintain focus on the instructional goal (Kolb, 2017).

We have structured this book around pedagogical content knowledge (PCK) (Shulman, 1987), but in this chapter, we find technological pedagogical content knowledge (TPCK) to be more appropriate (Koehler et al., 2014; Mishra & Koehler, 2006). In the same manner as

DOI: 10.4324/9781003274148-7

PCK, Mishra and Kohler understand the complex systems at play in a classroom and the necessity of a skillful blend of pedagogy and content that best suits student needs. However, technology can't just be tacked on to good instruction. The use of technology, too, must be best suited to the needs of the students and content. Instead of technology being an isolated element, TPCK addresses how teachers blend technology with pedagogy and content knowledge to best suit the content and students. It examines how the pedagogy of a lesson can integrate technology in constructive ways. Furthermore, TPCK looks at what makes content difficult or easy and students' prior knowledge to determine how technology can help students refine and deepen their understanding. This framework supports the notion that using technology in a classroom requires skill. Although the pandemic made almost all teachers online educators, to integrate technology into the classroom on a typical, daily basis, we need to consider how technology, content knowledge, and pedagogy come together to best meet the needs of the lesson.

At the same time, many teachers are not technology experts. Additionally, sometimes districts or schools mandate specific tools or devices that may not be what the classroom teacher would have selected. How do teachers wisely use technology in the classroom? Liz Kolb (2017) argues that technology must focus on a lesson's learning goals and be situated within strong instruction in order to be a useful tool. Her Triple E framework examines what this might look like in the classroom and can serve as a useful metric when you integrate new technologies into your instruction. It is designed to help teachers use technology in ways that enhance instruction and promote authentic learning.

Triple E has three levels: Engagement, Enhancement, and Extension (Kolb, 2020). The first dimension, Engagement, does not focus on the engagement with the technology but, really, the engagement in learning. When measuring engagement, teachers should consider if using the technology promotes time on task, motivates students to work on the lesson, and engages students actively with other learners. Level two, Enhancement, describes how the tool scaffolds learning in a way that could not be done without technology. Does it help students develop a more sophisticated understanding? Does it make the concept easier to understand? Does it offer a new way to demonstrate learning that could not be done without technology? The final level is Extension. This level is concerned with extending the learning beyond the classroom in order to connect with the real-world. At this level, we evaluate if technology can create a learning experience that is different from a normal school day, if it bridges a gap between the classroom and everyday life or if students can learn a life skill through using this technology. These guiding questions can help determine if incorporating technology into a lesson is appropriate or potentially distracting from the learning goal.

Additionally, Kolb (2020) has created scoring rubrics to help teachers evaluate technological tools, such as apps and websites, as well as lesson plans incorporating technology. Each of the guiding questions can be evaluated with a 0 for not at all, 1 for somewhat, and 2 for yes. Higher scores indicate the technology is having a positive impact on learning. More information about Triple E and the rubrics are available on her website: tripleeframework.com.

There are numerous technologies that can be used in the classroom. Oftentimes, teachers think of websites, apps, and digital creation tools. However, we would like to list a few that we find to be useful in social studies instruction and a bit less commonly found in classrooms.

Virtual Reality (VR)

VR immerses the user in a virtual environment. Oftentimes, this environment is three-dimensional and can be explored in 360 degrees. Numerous experiences are available online and can be used with or without a VR headset. Research has demonstrated that some users are more comfortable not using a headset, in which they can explore the environment using a handheld device (Hagan et al., 2020). It is less immersive this way but alleviates potential motion sickness and anxiety because users can simply put down the device and immediately stop the experience.

Augmented Reality (AR)

Augmented reality integrates digital elements or information into the real-world environment. It is not immersive, like VR, but superimposes computer-generated content onto a visual of the natural world. Sometimes these are delivered through a headset, onto a handheld device, or even an object.

Simulations and Models

Computer-based simulations demonstrate a process or response (*What is Computer Simulation*, n.d.). Simulations can offer opportunities to students in a safe, low-cost environment. For example, a chemistry simulation can allow students to explore what happens in a laboratory experiment without the risk of an adverse chemical reaction. Simulations can also mitigate the element of time. Programs like Oregon Trail, a westward migration game based in the 1800s, can give students the opportunity to explore what it was like to travel in a wagon train.

Geographic Information System (GIS) Maps

GIS maps merge location data and descriptive data on to a map (*What is GIS*, n.d). GIS maps often contain layers of information that you can turn on and off. For example, a city GIS map might have a layer for government, which displays city hall, the fire station, and the police station. Another layer might include schools and the library. A final layer may include stores and businesses. On the map, you can display all layers or single layers, depending on the information needed.

Digital Collections

Digital collections include digitally preserved files of various materials, such as images, manuscripts, books, newspapers, and documents (*What is a Digital Library*, n.d). These can offer a wealth of information, especially when looking for primary sources. Smithsonian Libraries, the Library of Congress, and the National Archives all have large digital collections.

Virtual Tours

Many museums, galleries, zoos, and aquariums as well as cities and historic sites offer virtual tours. These allow the user to explore their space and exhibits from a computer, usually for free. Some allow you to navigate the space yourself, while others include audio and visual elements. The Louvre, Georgia Aquarium, San Diego Zoo, Great Wall of China, and Smithsonian National Museum of Natural History are just a few of the places you can tour online.

The following inquiry lesson plan uses GIS maps and timelapse videos from Google Earth to better understand how humans impact the Earth. Students will explore some of the negative impacts humans have had on the Earth through climate change and the potential rising water levels. However, they will also see children around the world working to make a positive impact.

Content Knowledge

Before teaching this lesson, it is important that teachers have a firm grasp of human-environment interaction, including the positive and negative impacts humans have on Earth. Although it is impossible to have an exhaustive understanding of all impacts, there are a few that will be helpful to understand, such as climate change, global warming, pollution, re- and deforestation, renewable and nonrenewable energy, overpopulation, recycling, and environmental preserves and parks.

Resources About Human-Environment Interactions

1. **National Geographic: Human Impacts on the Environment Resource Library.** https://education.nationalgeographic.org/resource/resource-library-human-impacts-environment
   This site provides a database of videos, articles, and encyclopedia entries describing the positive and negative impacts humans have had on our planet.
2. **World Bank: Climate Change Portal**
   https://climateknowledgeportal.worldbank.org/overview
   Along with an informative article on climate change, this site provides compelling graphs and charts that display various impacts of climate change. The content of this site is somewhat technical.

3. **United Nations: What is Climate Change?**
www.un.org/en/climatechange/what-is-climate-change
Using everyday language, this site examines climate change, its global impacts, and its long-term effects.

4. **Understanding Global Change**
https://ugc.berkeley.edu/
This site provides slides presenting a model about global climate and environmental change. There are resources, which allow you to examine different factors and impacts of global change.

5. **Human Impact on the Environment**
https://scetv.pbslearningmedia.org/collection/climate-change-understanding-the-impact/
Videos, images, lesson plans, and documents are included in this database on human's impact on the environment.

6. **American Museum of Natural History: What You Can Do**
www.amnh.org/research/center-for-biodiversity-conservation/resources-and-publications/what-you-can-do
Focusing on steps individuals can take to reduce environmental impact, this site presents ways to help the Earth and combat climate change.

Pedagogy

Compelling Question: Can people change the Earth?

Objectives:

- Students will be able to explain what is shown in a GIS map.
- Students will be able to discuss one or more changes in the Earth over time.
- Students will be able to identify at least one way people have changed the Earth.
- Students will be able to support their thinking with evidence.

Throughout the lesson, we will reference graphic organizers. The "Inquiry Graphic Organizer" synthesizes the full lesson. It will be used at the beginning of the lesson for the compelling question and initial hypothesis. Then students will return to the Inquiry Graphic Organizer each time they complete a supporting question to record their findings and revised hypothesis. It will also be used when they write their final conclusion. The other graphic organizers, "Supporting Question __ Graphic Organizer," will support student inquiry for each of the supporting questions. As they investigate each question, students will complete the appropriate graphic organizer to record their findings for each source and their revised hypothesis. We find it helpful to fill in parts of each graphic organizer with the questions and sources before giving them to students. The graphic organizers for this lesson are provided at the end of the chapter.

Introduction

Activating Background Knowledge

Display the timelapse video on Google Earth: https://earth.app.goo.gl/KFTCjh. This page is a searchable map, which shows a Google Earth image from 1985 to 2020. Search for the location of your school and have the students watch the timelapse video. The video can be quick, so we suggest you and your students watch it multiple times and/or pause it periodically. You may also allow them to explore different locations on the timelapse map on their own devices.

As the students watch the video, ask:

- What do you notice?
  - If the students notice things on the map like "more brown areas" or "less green spaces," be sure to discuss what those green or brown areas show.
- Why do you think these changes occurred?
  - Students should conclude that, in many cases, people's activity caused the changes. If they are struggling to reach that conclusion, discuss some changes on the map individually and guide them to determine the causes of those changes and write them down. Then look at the list together and support them to make the generalization that those changes were caused by humans.

Note: It can take a long time to load the timelapse page. It would be a good idea to load it before the lesson begins.

Introduce Compelling Question

At this point in the lesson, don't discuss the compelling question much. Introduce the question "Can people change the Earth?" and remind students that the goal for this lesson is to answer this question. Give them the Inquiry Graphic Organizer to write the compelling question. Invite them to silently consider the question for a minute or two. Remind them to think about what they already know that might help them to answer this question.

Hypothesis

After thinking about the compelling question, have students write their initial hypothesis on their graphic organizer. Remind them that it is always good to provide evidence about their thinking but also to remember that this is their initial hypothesis, so it might be a guess at this point. As they continue in the lesson, they will gather more evidence to support their thinking. We recommend that students keep the Inquiry Graphic Organizer at their desk. After completing each station, ask students to return to their desk and revise their hypothesis on the Inquiry Graphic Organizer.

Instructional Procedures

This lesson is designed as a modified jigsaw activity. For supporting question 1, small groups will each look at one of the timelapse stories on Google Earth (https://earth.app.goo.gl/4vNJ7g): "Changing Forests," "Fragile Beauty," "Sources of Energy," "Warming Planet," and "Urban Expansion." Then the groups will share their findings by creating one or more slides for a presentation. For supporting questions 2 and 3, each small group will look at the same sources.

Supporting Question 1: How have humans impacted the Earth over time?
Source:

Timelapse in Google Earth
https://earth.app.goo.gl/4vNJ7g

There are several story maps included in the sidebar of the Google Earth timelapse. Assign each group one story map to the explore. They should read the slides and view the timelapse videos. Ask them to take notes on key evidence to answer the supporting question. Then create one or more slides reporting their evidence and answering the supporting question. Ask each group to present to the class. After viewing the presentations, ask students to revise their initial hypothesis using evidence from the timelapses.

Supporting Question 2: How do scientists think the world's oceans will change in the future if humans continue to have the same impact?
Sources:

1. NASA Climate Kids: How do we measure sea level?
    https://climatekids.nasa.gov/sea-level/
2. Google Earth: "Sea Levels and the Fate of Coastal Cities" https://earth.app.goo.gl/rSR3Gn

For this supporting question, start with NASA Climate Kids to better understand why sea levels rise and how it is measured. Have students explore the website and watch the video. Remind them to write notes about their learning to use as evidence and support when answering the question.

After students better understand why sea levels rise, have students visit the Google Earth site to explore the potential threat of rising sea levels on coastal cities. Be sure to explain to students that a rise of 2 degrees Celsius is the international target. Compare that to what might happen with a 4 degree increase. After reviewing both sites, ask students to look at their hypothesis again and revise it if their thinking has changed.

Supporting Question 3: Are all human impacts negative?
Source:

"A Better World with Jane Goodall's Roots & Shoots"
https://earth.app.goo.gl/mjG8vN

This story map tells about 11 groups of young people from around the world working with Jane Goodall's Roots & Shoots program to create change in their communities. As a class, read about some or all of the groups in the story map and discuss if and how they had a positive impact on the Earth. Remind students to write down evidence from the stories they read and to revise their hypothesis, if necessary, based on their evidence.

Conclusion

When everyone has completed all the centers, invite them back to revise their hypothesis of the compelling question one more time. Explain to them that this will be their conclusion, or final answer, for the compelling question. Also, remind them to reference their supporting questions and evidence from the centers. It might be helpful to model how to use evidence as support for their final conclusion, especially if this is one of the first times students are using primary sources within their inquiry to answer the compelling question. This can also be modelled after each center so students practice explaining their arguments using information from the primary sources.

Optional Extension

This inquiry project will likely spark student thinking about what they can do in their community to positively impact the Earth. We encourage you and your students to extend this project into community action or service learning. Begin by asking students if they know of ways they can make a positive impact on the Earth. This could be simple such as turning off the water while brushing their teeth or recycling. Students can track their positive impact practice in a log. Another option would be for students to work on creating awareness with others of how they can positively impact the Earth. The Roots & Shoots program, explored with the final supporting question, offers another option. Their program has a four-step process students can follow for identifying and addressing a local concern.

Adaptability and Differentiation

Early Childhood

For young children, we recommend viewing each of the sources as a class. Focus on the images and how they change. Teachers may need to give young children more scaffolding, but we encourage teachers to engage them in deep thinking about the changes in the world. Asking them about differences they notice, changing colors on the maps, or what happens when it rains a lot are accessible to young children and can spark good discussion. Also, we recommend doing the first supporting question together and breaking this inquiry into several sessions, as each source has a lot of information.

Middle Level

Middle school students may be able to create their own additional supporting questions focusing on science content that overlaps with social studies content, thus providing for interdisciplinary options. For example, the Next Generation Science Standards (National Research Council, 2013) have middle school sections on ecosystems and Earth and human activity. Middle school students can write supporting questions that tie into both science and social studies content and then research for evidence to answer their questions.

Students with Special Needs

Although this inquiry is mostly map based, there is also a lot of text. We suggest using screen-reading programs for struggling readers or for the teacher to read it to the class. Also, students with ADHD may have a difficult time focusing with all of the information, maps, and options. If possible, the teacher may need to guide the process rather than allow students to explore the sites on their own.

Inquiry Graphic Organizer

Compelling Question:

Can people change the Earth?

Hypothesis:

Supporting Question 1:	Supporting Question 2:	Supporting Question 3:
How have humans impacted the Earth over time?	How do scientists think the world's oceans will change in the future if humans continue to have the same impact?	Are all human impacts negative?

Findings:	Findings:	Findings:
Revised Hypothesis:	Revised Hypothesis:	Revised Hypothesis:

Final Conclusion (should answer CQ and use evidence):

Additional Notes:

Figure 5.1 "Can people change the earth?" Inquiry Graphic Organizer

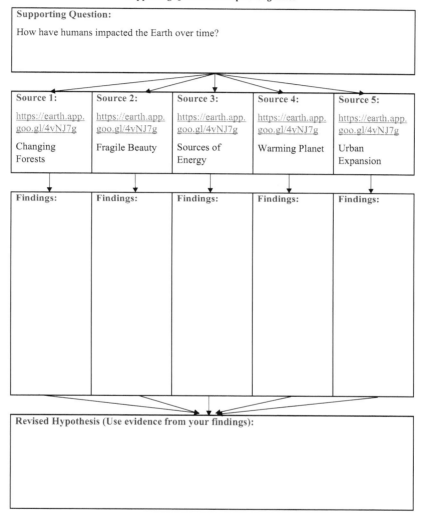

Figure 5.2 "How have humans impacted the Earth over time?" Supporting Question 1 Graphic Organizer

Supporting Question 2 Graphic Organizer

Supporting Question: How do scientists think the world's oceans will change in the future if humans continue to have the same impact?

Source 1:	Source 2:
NASA ClimateKids: How do we measure sea level? https://climatekids.nasa.gov/sea-level/	Google Earth: "Sea Levels and the Fate of Coastal Cities" https://earth.app.goo.gl/rSR3Gn

Findings:	Findings:

Revised Hypothesis (Use evidence from your findings):

Figure 5.3 "How do scientists think the world's oceans will change in the future if humans continue to have the same impact?" Supporting Question 2 Graphic Organizer

Supporting Question 3 Graphic Organizer

Supporting Question: Are all human impacts negative?

↓

Source: "A Better World with Jane Goodall's Roots & Shoots"   https://earth.app.goo.gl/mjG8vN

↓

Findings:

↓

Revised Hypothesis (Use evidence from your findings):

Figure 5.4 "Are all human impacts negative?" Supporting Question 3 Graphic Organizer

References

Hagan, H. N., Fegely, A., & Warriner, G., III. (2020). Virtual reality in C3 inquiry. *Social Studies and the Young Learner, 32*(4).

Koehler, M. J., Mishra, P., Kereluik, K., Shin, T. S., & Graham, C. R. (2014). The technological pedagogical content knowledge framework. In *Handbook of research on educational communications and technology* (4th ed., pp. 101–111). Springer.

Kolb, L. (2017). *Learning first, technology second: The educator's guide to designing authentic lessons.* International Society for Tech in Ed.

Kolb, L. (2020). *Triple E framework.* Triple E Framework. Retrieved September 29, 2022, from www.tripleeframework.com/

Mishra, P., & Koehler, M. J. (2006). Technological pedagogical content knowledge: A framework for teacher knowledge. *Teachers College Record, 108*(6), 1017–1054. https://doi.org/10.1111/j.1467-9620.2006.00684.

National Research Council. (2013). *Next generation science standards: For states, by states.* The National Academies Press. https://doi.org/10.17226/18290.

Shulman, L. (1987). Knowledge and teaching: Foundations of the new reform. *Harvard Educational Review, 57*(1), 1–23. https://doi.org/10.17763/haer.57.1.j463w79r56455411

What is a Computer Simulation? – Definition from Techopedia. (n.d.). *Techopedia.com.* Retrieved September 29, 2022, from www.techopedia.com/definition/17060/computer-simulation

What is a Digital Collection or Digital Library? (n.d.). *Anderson archival.* Retrieved September 29, 2022, from https://andersonarchival.com/learn/what-is-a-digital-collection-or-digital-library/

What is GIS? | Geographic Information System Mapping Technology. (n.d.). Retrieved September 29, 2022, from www.esri.com/en-us/what-is-gis/overview

6

INTEGRATING LITERATURE

Introduction to Approach

Over the last 20 years, social studies has become more and more endangered in the elementary classroom. Teachers who have been told that literacy and math take priority have trouble finding time in the school day for anything else (Boyle-Baise et al., 2008). This is especially true when both literacy and math have long "blocks" of time devoted to them. Social studies may end up on the schedule for the last 30 minutes of the day (frequently rotated with science) and that means it may never happen or that students are too tired to focus on social studies.

One way that teachers try to combat the erosion of social studies is through integration with literature. Heafner (2018) wrote about a school, which recommended that social studies be integrated with literacy. However, she found "Integration, while viewed to be the most effective method for teaching social studies in this context, was underutilized,

DOI: 10.4324/9781003274148-8

misunderstood and varied widely. The resulting outcomes for social studies were far from what was intended" (p. 6). Similarly, Huck (2019) found that teachers need more information about how to integrate social studies and literacy well.

One problem with how teachers integrate social studies and literacy is that social studies is only used as the topic for the reading without delving into the historical or democratic thinking. For example, Boyle-Baise et al. (2008) observed a class where students read a passage about Nazism and then answered questions about the reading. Unfortunately, the questions were all focused on reading comprehension and there was no critical examination of the reading. Social studies became a recitation of facts that students read with no consideration of social studies processes.

Using children's literature as part of inquiry stations can help teachers integrate social studies and literacy in more meaningful ways. The lesson outlined in the next section has students reading through children's literature about article 23 of the UN Universal Declaration of Human Rights (UDHR) focusing on the right to join trade unions, which in turn leads to the right of "favourable conditions of work" (UDHR, n.d., article 23). While the lesson focuses on the social studies aspects of integration, teachers could easily match reading standards from their grade level to the children's books listed. The selection in the next section is a mixture of both nonfiction and historical fiction.

In addition to using children's literature to integrate literacy and social studies, An (2021a, 2021b) wrote about how it can be used to teach elementary students about difficult history, challenge dominant narratives, and connect history to the present. For example, she wrote about using Korean children's literature to teach students about the Korean War (2021a). She also wrote about using children's books about the Philippines to teach about the US history of colonization, therefore, challenging the dominant narrative of US foreign policy. She describes difficult knowledge as "social and historical content that carries an emotional burden for students and teachers because the content often involves state-sanctioned violence, refutes dominant socio historical narratives, and thus creates feelings of discomfort or unease" (An, 2021b, p. 11).

Finally, using children's literature in inquiry can help students make connections between the past and present. Ferreras-Stone and Demoiny (2019) connect the history of protest marches to current examples, such as Black Lives Matter and March for Our Lives, by using four-picture books. They have an overarching theme concerning what it means to be a citizen and what activities citizens participate in. Doing focused, critical inquiry showing the similarities with past movements can help students make connections and challenge dominant narratives.

The following inquiry lesson focuses on the UDHR, specifically how the document guarantees rights about work. These rights include favorable working conditions and the right to join a union. In this lesson, students learn about the history of labor movements in the United States through stations that feature children's literature. Then during the final conclusion, students learn about current labor movements. The lesson starts with an introduction to the UDHR and then focuses specifically on article 23.

Content Knowledge

An inquiry into the UDHR can be written to encompass an overview of the entire document or it can focus on specific articles. This inquiry lesson could easily be reframed to focus on voting rights, education, marriage/family, or fair trial. There are children's books about each of these topics and about the UDHR more generally. The focus on this lesson, however, is on article 23, which states:

> Article 23: (1) Everyone has the right to work, to free choice of employment, to just and favourable conditions of work and to protection against unemployment. (2) Everyone, without any discrimination, has the right to equal pay for equal work. (3) Everyone who works has the right to just and favourable remuneration ensuring for himself and his family an existence worthy of human dignity, and supplemented, if necessary, by other means of social protection. (4) Everyone has the right to form and to join trade unions for the protection of his interests.

Resources specific to the labor movement in the United States:

1. *American workers series:* **The Homestead Steel Strike of 1892; The Pullman Strike of 1894; The Ludlow Massacre of 1913–14; Mother Jones; Cesar Chavez; The Bread and Roses Strike of 1912**
   These books detail several different worker's rights movements. They can be read by students, particularly older students, but also provide background information that can help teachers.

2. *CSPAN: Cities Tour-Labor Movement in the U.S.,* **www.c-span.org/video/?508236-1/cities-tour-labor-movement-us**
   This documentary traces the US labor movement through different times and places across the United States.

3. *Kids on Strike* **by Susan Campbell Bartoletti**
   This book has seven chapters, each focusing on a different strike involving children's rights between 1836 and 1912. It includes pictures and descriptions.

4. **NBC NEWS: The Rise of Labor Unions: www.youtube.com/watch?v=2xrnu_7dRrY**
   This brief video shares the history of the US labor unions, specifically during the Industrial Revolution.

5. **Timeline of labor movements in US: www.pbs.org/wgbh/americanexperience/features/theminewars-labor-wars-us/**
   This site contains an informative timeline that traces the US labor movement from 1874 to 1989.

One of the most difficult parts of planning an inquiry that uses children's literature is finding appropriate, well-written children's literature. There are a couple of good lists to start with:

1. **NCSS Notable Trade Books,** www.socialstudies.org/notable-trade-books
   Notable Trade Books are awarded each year for their outstanding social studies content and high literary value. These books are written for K–12 readers.

2. **Carter G. Woodson Award Winners,** www.socialstudies.org/get-involved/carter-g-woodson-book-award-and-honor-winners
   Each year, the Carter G. Woodson Award is given to an elementary, middle, and secondary winner and honoree. The award is for books, which depict ethnicity in the United States.

3. **Coretta Scott King Award Winners,** www.ala.org/rt/emiert/cskbookawards
   The Coretta Scott King Award, selected by the American Library
   Association, is given to an outstanding book that is written or illus-
   trated by an African American and depicts African American culture.
4. **Social Justice Books: Booklists,** https://socialjusticebooks.org/booklists/
   This site has numerous critically reviewed booklists for various topics or cultures, such as gentrification, Arabs and Arab Americans,
   and body positivity.
5. **Learning for Justice: Student Texts,** www.learningforjustice.org/
   classroom-resources/texts
   Learning for Justice's entire site is dedicated to working towards
   racial justice. The Student Texts page includes various medias that
   can be used for students of different ages. The selected texts meet
   the Learning for Justice Social Justice Standards and can be filtered
   to focus on children's books.

Finally, local children's librarians and school librarians are a wonderful
resource for finding children's books.

Pedagogy

Compelling Question: How do people fight for favorable working conditions in the United States?

Objectives:

- Students will be able to explain the purpose of the UDHR and list at
  least one of its rights.
- Students will be able to gather information from children's books to
  answer questions.
- Students will be able to describe the labor movement throughout US
  history.
- Students will be able to compare historic and recent labor movements in the United States.

Throughout the lesson, we will reference graphic organizers. The
"Inquiry Graphic Organizer" synthesizes the full lesson. It will be used

at the beginning of the lesson for the compelling question and initial hypothesis. Then students will return to the Inquiry Graphic Organizer each time they complete a supporting question to record their findings and revised hypothesis. It will also be used when they write their final conclusion. The other graphic organizers, "Supporting Question ___ Graphic Organizer," will support student inquiry for each of the supporting questions. As they investigate each question, students will complete the appropriate graphic organizer to record their findings for each source and their revised hypothesis. We find it helpful to fill in parts of each graphic organizer with the questions and sources before giving them to students. The graphic organizers for this lesson are provided at the end of the chapter.

Introduction

Activating Background Knowledge

To introduce the UDHR, show this video: www.youtube.com/ watch?v=uA1IZkWycMk. Then divide students into small groups and assign each group one of the articles, sharing the corresponding section of this pdf: www.un.org/en/udhrbook/pdf/udhr_booklet_en_web.pdf. Once students are in small groups and read their assigned article, students should create a picture to explain their assigned right.

When everyone has completed and presented their picture explaining individual rights in the UDHR, point out that we have a right to "favorable working conditions." Discuss what that means and what workers can do if conditions are not favorable.

Read *Click, Clack, Moo: Cows that Type* by Doreen Cronin, which is about animals that do not have favorable working conditions. After reading, discuss those conditions and how the animals convinced the farmer to make changes. Explain that they are going to read more books about when people in the United States have had unfavorable working conditions and how they worked together to make changes.

Introduce Compelling Question

At this point in the lesson, don't discuss the compelling question much. Introduce the question "How do people fight for favorable working conditions in the United States?" and remind students that the goal for this lesson is to answer this question. Give them the Inquiry Graphic Organizer to write the compelling question. Invite them to silently consider the question for a minute or two. Remind them to think about what they already know that might help them to answer this question.

Hypothesis

After thinking about the compelling question, have students write their initial hypothesis on their graphic organizer. Remind them that it is always good to provide evidence about their thinking but also to remember that this is their initial hypothesis, so it might be a guess at this point. As they continue in the lesson, they will gather more evidence to support their thinking. We recommend that students keep the Inquiry Graphic Organizer at their desk. After completing each station, ask students to return to their desk and revise their hypothesis on the Inquiry Graphic Organizer.

Instructional Procedures

After students have had the opportunity to write their hypothesis, introduce each of the stations in the next section. We have listed several selections for each supporting question. Select the book(s), which are available and most appropriate for your students and context. After each station, make sure students have an opportunity to revise their hypotheses on their graphic organizers. Instead of stations, these can also be completed as a whole class with the teacher reading each book or a selection of books for each topic.

Supporting Question 1: What were working conditions like in the early 1900s in factories? How did these conditions lead to strikes?
Sources:

1. *Flesh and Blood So Cheap: The Triangle Fire and Its Legacy* by Albert Marrin
   This book goes through the history of the Triangle Shirtwaist Factory fire. It's very long, so for the purpose of this station, students only need to read the prologue.

2. *Fannie Never Flinched: One Woman's Courage in the Struggle for American Labor Union Rights* by Mary Cronk Farrell

   This book tells the story of Fannie Mooney Sellins, a member and later president of the United Garment Workers of America. This includes stories of other unions in the late 1800s/early 1900s

3. *Brave Girl: Clara and the Shirtwaist Maker's Strike of 1909* by Michelle Markey

   This book tells the story of Clara Lemlich, a recent immigrant who helps to organize garment workers to go on strike in the early 1900s.

4. *Audacity* by Melanie Crowder*

   This is another book about Clara Lemlich, but it is written as poems and somewhat fictionalized. There is a historical note at the end that can be very helpful for students. This book would be better for older readers.

5. *Uprising* by Margaret Peterson Haddix*

   This is a historical fiction novel about the Triangle Shirtwaist Factory fire in 1911. It would be best for older students.

6. *Bread and Roses, Too* by Katherine Paterson*

   This historical fiction novel focuses on the mill strikes of 1912. The main character's father died in a mill accident. Her family is participating in the strike, but she is sent away for her safety.

*These last three are novels and may need to be read in advance or just use selections.

Once students have read and discussed the sources, have them answer the supporting question using evidence from the sources. After that, they should return to their hypothesis and revise it according to their learning.

Supporting Question 2: What were working conditions like in the early 1900s in mines? How did these conditions lead to strikes?
Sources:

1. *Mother Jones and Her Army of Mill Children* by Jonah Winter and Nancy Carpenter

   This is a picture book about the children's march of 1903 organized by Mother Jones to highlight children's working conditions.

2. *On Our Way to Oyster Bay: Mother Jones and Her March for Children's Rights* by Monica Kulling and Felicita Sala

   This is another picture book about the children's march of 1903. It goes into a little more depth than the first one.

3. *Breaker Boys: How a Photograph Helped End Child Labor* by Michael Burgan
   This is an in-depth look of coal mining conditions in the early 1900s. It has several pictures and explanations throughout.

Once students have read and discussed the sources, have them answer the supporting question using evidence from the sources. After that, they should return to their hypothesis and revise it according to their learning.

Supporting Question 3: How did workers fight for fair working conditions in the mid-1990s? How were conditions the same and different in cities and farms?

Sources:

1. *Memphis, Martin, and the Mountaintop: The Sanitation Strike of 1968* by Alice Faye Duncan
   This book is about the sanitation strike in Memphis in 1968. It is told from the perspective of the daughter of a sanitation worker.
2. *Strike!: The Farm Workers' Fight for Their Rights* by Larry Dane Brimner
   This book is about the farm workers' strike of the 1960s. It's pretty in depth, so you may only be able to use snippets or short sections.
3. *Harvesting Hope: The Story of Cesar Chavez* by Kathleen Krull and Yuyi Morales
   This picture book is a biography of Cesar Chavez's life. It includes information about his leading of the farm workers' strikes.
4. *Dolores Huerta: A Hero to Migrant Workers* by Sarah Warren and Robert Casilla
   This picture book tells the story of Dolores Huerta and her fight to help organize migrant workers during the mid-twentieth century.
5. *Up Molasses Mountain* by Julie Baker
   This is a novel about the West Virginia coal miners' strike of the 1950s.

Once students have read and discussed the sources, have them answer the supporting question using evidence from the sources. After that, they should return to their hypothesis and revise it according to their learning.

Supporting Question 4: What were working conditions like in the early 2000s? How did these conditions lead to strikes?

Source:

1. *¡Si, Se Puede!/Yes, We Can!: Janitor Strike in L.A.* by Diana Cohn
   This book is about the successful janitor strike in LA in 2000. It is told through the perspective of the son of a striker.

2. *Undocumented: A Worker's Fight* by Duncan Tonatiuh
    This is the story of undocumented workers fighting for fair wages.

Once students have read and discussed the sources, have them answer the supporting question using evidence from the sources. After that, they should return to their hypothesis and revise it according to their learning.

Conclusion

After students have revised their hypothesis for the last time, ask students to share responses to the compelling question: How do people fight for favorable working conditions in the United States? Encourage them to use examples from history that they learned in their stations.

Then discuss what students think would be considered unfavorable working conditions today. Then the class can make a list on the board. Finally, choose one or two news stories about recent strikes to share with students.

Note: Here are a few recent news stories from 2019 to 2022. However, if these are not timely or meaningful to your context, you should be able to find other current or local examples. We suggest searching online and looking at national and local news media sites.

1. NBC NEWS: *Thousands of John Deere Workers Go On Strike,* www.youtube.com/watch?v=MCHZU_BTnAc
2. NPR: *Understanding America's Teachers Strikes,* www.youtube.com/watch?v=5l-WrfOTHfA
3. CNN: *Amazon Workers Celebrate First Labor Union,* www.cnn.com/videos/business/2022/04/04/amazon-labor-union-new-york-hln-vpx.cnnbusiness
4. *Vox: How a Bunch of Starbucks Baristas Built a Labor Movement,* www.vox.com/recode/22993509/starbucks-successful-union-drive

Revisit their list of current unfavorable working conditions and compare the students' initial thoughts with what they learned in the news stories. Then create a Venn diagram comparing the historical events to those in recent times. This may be done as a class or by assigning one historical event and one recent event to small groups. Conclude the session by asking if people today fight for favorable working conditions in the same ways they did throughout history.

Optional Extension

To extend this inquiry, students can also consider the rights given to workers through each event. We encourage teachers and students to create a public awareness campaign about how workers have accomplished change in the US and what conditions are now protected because of them. This might take the form of hallway posters in their school, a website, or museum exhibits, where they serve as docents.

Adaptability and Differentiation

Early Childhood

For early childhood, the teacher will definitely need to read the books to the class. Teachers will also probably need to explain vocabulary, possibly doing more in the early stages of the lessons to prepare students for words they may have never heard before. Because some of the books are novels designed for older readers, teachers could either just focus on the picture books or read small snippets from the novels.

Middle Level

For middle-level students, it might be best to assign a few of the novels over a couple of days or assign them to different literature circles. Students can answer the supporting questions as they read the novels. They also could create their own supporting questions as they read the longer novels and nonfiction books.

Students with Special Needs

Many of these books can be found as audiobooks, and several have videos of them being read on YouTube. It is also possible to record yourself reading the book in advance so students can watch along in different groups. It may also be beneficial to only use small sections of the books instead of the entire book for this lesson.

Inquiry Graphic Organizer

Compelling Question:

How do people fight for favorable working conditions in the United States?

Hypothesis:

Supporting Question 1:	Supporting Question 2:	Supporting Question 3:	Supporting Question 4:
What were working conditions like in the early 1900s in factories? How did these conditions lead to strikes?	What were working conditions like in the early 1900s in mines? How did these conditions lead to strikes?	How did workers fight for fair working conditions in the mid 1900s? How were conditions the same and different in cities and farms?	What were working conditions like in the early 2000s? How did these conditions lead to strikes?

Findings:	Findings:	Findings:	Findings:
Revised Hypothesis:	**Revised Hypothesis:**	**Revised Hypothesis:**	**Revised Hypothesis:**

Final Conclusion (should answer CQ and use evidence):

Additional Notes:

Figure 6.1 "How do people fight for favorable working conditions in the United States?" Inquiry Graphic Organizer

Supporting Question 1 Graphic Organizer

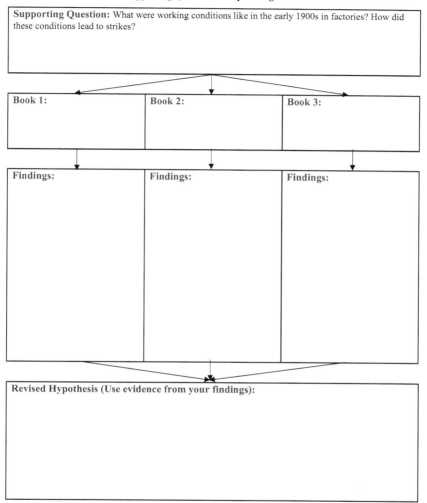

Figure 6.2 "What were working conditions like in the early 1900s in factories? How did these conditions lead to strikes?" Supporting Question 1 Graphic Organizer

Supporting Question 2 Graphic Organizer

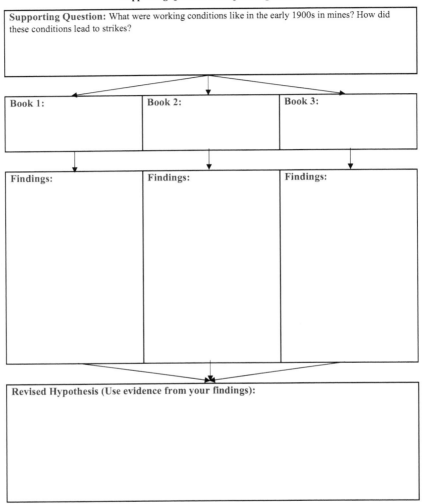

Figure 6.3 "What were working conditions like in the early 1900s in mines? How did these conditions lead to strikes?" Supporting Question 2 Graphic Organizer

Supporting Question 3 Graphic Organizer

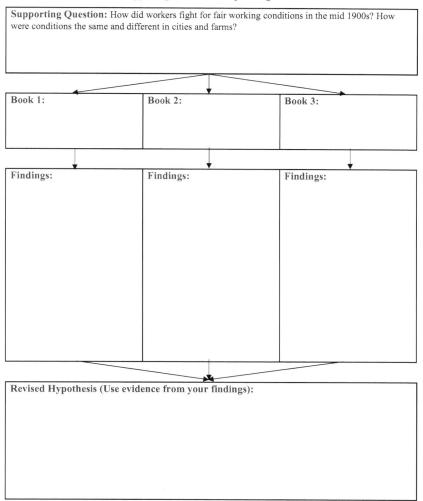

Figure 6.4 "How did workers fight for fair working conditions in the mid 1900s? How were conditions the same and different in cities and farms?" Supporting Question 3 Graphic Organizer

Supporting Question 4 Graphic Organizer

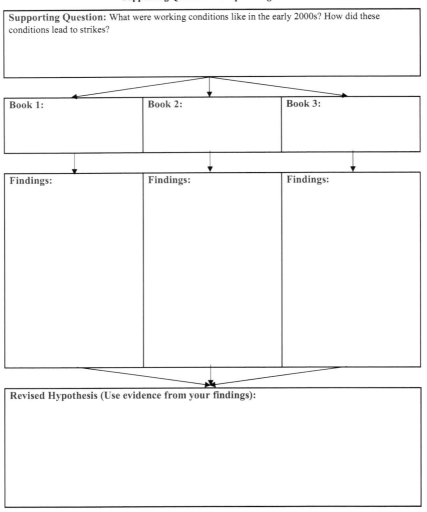

Figure 6.5 "What were working conditions like in the early 2000s? How did these conditions lead to strikes?" Supporting Question 4 Graphic Organizer

References

An, S. (2021a). Teaching difficult knowledge of the Korean War through international children's literature. *Social Studies and the Young Learner, 33*(3), 24–32.

An, S. (2021b). Teaching difficult knowledge of World War II in the Philippines with children's literature and inquiry. *Social Studies and the Young Learner, 34*(1), 10–15.

Boyle-Baise, M., Hsu, M. C., Johnson, S., Serriere, S. C., & Stewart, D. (2008). Putting reading first: Teaching social studies in elementary classrooms. *Theory & Research in Social Education, 36*(3), 233–255. https://doi.org/10.1080/00933104.2008.10473374

Ferreras-Stone, J., & Demoiny, S. B. (2019). Why are people marching? Discussing justice-oriented citizenship using picture books. *Social Studies and the Young Learner, 32*(1), 3–9.

Heafner, T. L. (2018). Elementary ELA/SS integration: Challenges and limitations. *The Social Studies, 109*(1), 1–12. https://doi.org/10.1080/00377996.2017.1399248

Huck, A. (2019). Elementary social studies content integration in CCLS: An analysis of content integration. *The Social Studies, 110*(1), 1–16. https://doi.org/10.1080/00377996.2018.1524359

Universal Declaration of Human Rights. (n.d.). *Amnesty international.* Retrieved May 19, 2022, from www.amnesty.org/en/what-we-do/universal-declaration-of-human-rights/

7

UTILIZING CIVIC AGENCY

Introduction to Approach

Throughout this book, we consider the purpose of social studies to be the preparation of future citizens, and inquiry-based instruction equips students with a variety of skills and tools to use in that role. According to NCSS (n.d.), the goal is to "promote civic competence [and] to help young people develop the ability to make informed and reasoned decisions for the public good as citizens of a culturally diverse, democratic society in an interdependent world." Commonly, these skills are referred to as "civic efficacy" (Serriere, 2005). However, we argue that citizens should not simply be knowledgeable but also civically engaged and develop a sense of agency. Civic agency is an individual's understanding that they have a voice and that it can make a difference (Serriere, 2005). It is not just knowing that a citizen can make a difference but an understanding that they, themselves, can take action and impact change for what they believe in.

DOI: 10.4324/9781003274148-9

Students, however, do not necessarily see themselves as having an impact on the world around them. They may have a narrow view of citizenship that focuses on voting or simply doing the right thing. Others may think they are too young to have an impact. We do not expect children to enter the classroom with a sense of their agency but, instead, see civic participation as a learned act (Silva Dias & Menezes, 2014). Classroom experiences can, and should, give children the opportunities to expand their conceptions of citizen to include their own voice and action.

Furthermore, Silva Dias and Menezes (2014) write that "children and adolescents' experiences in their life contexts, such as family and school—but not limited to these—emerge as central to the development of political thought and citizenship conceptions." Schools make an ideal setting for children to develop and use their voice for change. It is a lived context, where children collaborate, work, and exchange ideas with others who differ from themselves. Schools must make space to foster civic thinking and model democratic practices.

Throughout the school day, students engage in civic spaces and exercise agency informally (Hauver, 2017). While working with children in several schools, Hauver found that students navigate their spaces. In their contexts, students develop ideas about how to engage with others as community members. They may not realize they are engaging civically, but they begin to form understandings about "appropriate" discourses, whose voices matter, and who are insiders or outsiders. Furthermore, data indicates that when students collaborate, their civic understandings deepen (Hauver, 2017).

Formal civic learning is also taking place in classrooms through experiences, such as student government, service learning, and simulations (Blevins et al., 2016). Considering that taking action is the fourth dimension of the C3 framework and that it is a core aspect of citizenship, developing civic agency is an important classroom goal. Students need to understand that they can act for change and make a difference. At the same time, it is missing from many classrooms. It is easy to complete a lesson or inquiry without engaging in action or sharing learning in a meaningful way. Sometimes there is not enough time, and other times, teachers may not know how to start. Without a specific objective for civic action or to develop agency, learning seems to occur without taking action. We encourage teachers not to skip that step. Learning to communicate learning and take action is an important step in developing civic agency.

This lesson presents a first step into students identifying their agency and ways to exercise it. It is situated in the students' lived contexts, in their spaces with the issues that they identify. First, the class hears from a Sudanese "lost boy," who founded an organization, which brings water to villages. His experiences show how an "average" person can identify a need and implement change. From there, students see more examples of everyday people that have made a difference. Then they each identify communities they are a part of, needs in that community, and steps needed to make change. Finally, they develop, and hopefully share, their plan of action. Throughout the inquiry, they continue to develop their sense of agency to determine where and how they can make an impact in their everyday lives.

Content Knowledge

Teachers and students might want to read biographies or view documentaries to learn more about people who have used their agency. However, because this lesson is based on students' lived experiences, the best background knowledge for teachers is an understanding of their students. Building connections with each student and developing a knowledge of their identity and communities will strengthen a teacher's ability to facilitate the inquiry and support students.

Pedagogy

Compelling Question: What Can I do with My Agency?

Objectives:

- Students will identify examples of ordinary citizens who took action for change.
- Students will be able to engage in inquiry to answer the compelling question: What can I do with my agency?
- Students will be able to collaboratively create an action plan for change based on their own sense of agency and identified needs.

Throughout the lesson, we will reference graphic organizers. The "Inquiry Graphic Organizer" synthesizes the full lesson. It will be used at the beginning of the lesson for the compelling question and initial hypothesis. Then students will return to the Inquiry Graphic Organizer each time they complete a supporting question to record their findings and revised hypothesis. It will also be used when they write their final conclusion. The other graphic organizers, "Supporting Question __ Graphic Organizer," will support student inquiry for each of the supporting questions. As they investigate each question, students will complete the appropriate graphic organizer to record their findings for each source and their revised hypothesis. We find it helpful to fill in parts of each graphic organizer with the questions and sources before giving them to students. The graphic organizers for this lesson are provided at the end of the chapter.

Introduction

Activating Background Knowledge

Ask students if they are aware of ordinary people who enacted extraordinary changes. (Students might suggest Malala, Greta Thunburg, or Rosa Parks.) After a brief discussion, show this clip of Salva Dut speaking with a group of children about his experiences in Sudan: *https://youtu.be/D33I3Uqr8VE*. Salva is one of the "lost boys" of Sudan, the founder of the organization Water for South Sudan, and the focus of the true story *A Long Walk to Water* by L.S. Park. After watching the clip, discuss how Salva made a difference in his community and then discuss how the class can make changes in the community.

Introduce the inquiry by explaining that the class will focus on agency today. Agency, in this context, is the power citizens can use to make change. When we first think about how we can make change, we need to spend time thinking about who we are, then focus on people who have made a difference. Next, we will investigate where we can advocate for change and, finally, discuss how we can advocate for change.

Introduce Compelling Question

At this point in the lesson, don't discuss the compelling question much. Introduce the question "What can I do with my agency?" and remind students that the goal for this lesson is to answer this question. Give them the Inquiry Graphic Organizer to write the compelling question. Invite them to silently consider the question for a minute or two. Remind them to think about what they already know that might help them to answer this question.

Hypothesis

After thinking about the compelling question, have students write their initial hypothesis on their graphic organizer. Remind them that it is always good to provide evidence about their thinking but also to remember that this is their initial hypothesis, so it might be a guess at this point. As they continue in the lesson, they will gather more evidence to support their thinking. We recommend that students keep the Inquiry Graphic Organizer at their desk. After completing each station, ask students to return to their desk and revise their hypothesis on the Inquiry Graphic Organizer.

Instructional Procedures

Supporting Question 1: Are there others like me?
Source:

1. Students will read excerpts from the book *Stories for Kids Who Dare to be Different: True Tales of Amazing People Who Stood Up and Stood Out* by Ben Brooks.

Recommended stories include:

   a. Loujain Al-Hathloul (page 12): Loujain fought the law forbidding women from driving in Saudi Arabia.

   b. Luke Amber (page 15): After his brother committed suicide, Luke started an organization to provide a safe space for men to talk about feelings in order to remove the stigma of talking about mental health issues.

   c. Jamie Chadwick (page 43): Jamie was the first woman to win the British GT Championship car race. She challenged stereotypes that women could not race cars.

   d. Jessica Cox (page 48): Jessica was born without arms but learned to fly a plane, along with earning black belts in taekwondo and participating in various sports.

e. Liam Davis (page 52): Liam was one of the first openly gay soccer players in the Premier League of England.

f. Kelvin Doe (page 64): Kelvin was born in Freetown, Sierra Leone. He did not always have electricity, but he was able to use what he could find to create generators, battery power lamps, and sound mixers. He moved to Canada and started his own company making solar-powered light and a long-lasting phone charger.

g. Greta Gerwig (page 72): Greta wanted to become an actress and make movies. She was not accepted to any acting school. Instead, she began to make her own films with her friends until she started being cast in larger productions. Eventually, she made her own film about her early life and it was nominated for an Oscar.

h. Savanna Karmue (page 91): Savanna founded an organization to educate people on heart disease prevention.

i. Sophie Pascoe (page 112): Sophie lost a leg in a childhood accident. She won several medals in the 2008 Paralympics when she was only 15 years old.

j. Eric Underwood (page 148): Eric is a star for the Royal Ballet. He had to overcome prejudice as an African American male interested in ballet.

2. Teachers can also use podcasts to differentiate sources for students. These two have selections which can be used:
    a. Podcast: www.rebelgirls.com/pages/podcast
    b. Big Life Kids Podcast: https://biglifejournal.com/blogs/podcast

Supporting Question 2: Where do I belong?
Source:

Teachers will start by explaining that in order to use their agency, students first must discover what their agency is. In this section, students will focus on where they could have influence. Students will answer the questions in the next section about where they fit in their school and in their community.

Ask students to identify their place, with several questions, guiding them to identify their sphere of influence. Teachers can tailor the list to their school and community context and provide scaffolding according to student need. Guiding questions might include the following:

1. Where do I belong at school?
    a. Grade?
    b. Clubs?
    c. Sports teams?
    d. Friends?
    e. Leadership (such as student council, mentoring, etc.)?
2. Where do I belong in the community?
    a. Teams?
    b. Clubs and organizations (such as 4-H, Scouts, etc.)?
    c. Religious groups?
    d. Neighborhood?
    e. The arts (such as piano lessons, children's symphony, community theater, etc.)?

Supporting Question 3: What do I see as a need?
Source:

This part of the activity can be done individually or in small groups. The younger the student, the more time they might need to discuss in small groups. Older students might start individually, then move to small groups. Students will meet in small groups and discuss what they see as needs in their school or community. Teachers can provide guidance, such as thinking of your spheres of influence from question 1: What do you see as areas of need in your school groups or community groups?

Some examples could include the following:

a. In our neighborhood, the road leading to my house has a lot of litter.
b. The city is planning to change the road outside of school from one way to two way, and we are worried about our safety as we arrive at school.
c. Social distancing on the playground makes it so that the fastest students get to use the best playground equipment every day for all of recess.

d. If students are having trouble thinking of ideas, they can research local nonprofit groups as well as local newspapers for ideas of needs in their community.

Students (individually or in groups) create a list of possible changes that are needed. Finally, as a whole class, students work to decide which changes the class can advocate for. (This can be one project for the entire class or smaller projects for groups or individuals.)

Supporting Question 4: What steps are necessary to make changes for that need?

Source:

Once students decide on a project, they can divide into groups and brainstorm ways they could make the change they identified.

Conclusion

Finally, students will create an action plan for their project to answer the compelling question "What can I do with my agency?" In step four, they identified the steps they need to take. During the conclusion, they work with the teacher to solidify how to complete those steps. For example, if they have decided they need more playground equipment to solve the problems caused by social distancing, they would work with the teacher to figure out how to make that happen (who to talk to, how to raise money, etc.).

Adaptability and Differentiation

Early Childhood

Students in preschool and early grades have agency in a variety of contexts but may have difficulty identifying those. With this age, the lesson would work better when done as a class. For the second question, the class can identify groups they are all a part of, such as their class, school, and grade level. Then they can identify and work on an issue in those contexts together. For example, they may decide that the hallway to their classroom should be more welcoming and, after listing several ideas, decide to make art and signs to decorate it for each season.

Middle Level

For middle school students, the examples used for supporting question 1 may feel childish. Instead of using a single book, we have compiled a list of young people students could research to determine how they made an impact.

1. Greta Thurnberg
2. Malala Yousafzai
3. Gitanjali Rao
4. Claudette Colvin
5. Avi Schiffman
6. Xiuhtezcatl Martinez
7. Louis Braille
8. Emma Gonzalez
9. Param Jaggi
10. Marley Dias
11. Easton LaChappelle
12. Melati and Isabel Wijsen
13. Nicholas Lowinger
14. Jaylen Arnold
15. Jazz Jennings
16. Thandiwe Chama
17. Ann Makosinski

Students with Special Needs

This lesson's activities can be differentiated in a variety of ways. In the opening of the lesson, there is information about Salva Dut available in a variety of forms – written, audio, and video. There are also videos and podcasts about children who have made a difference that can be used as examples for supporting question 1. Student responses may take a variety of forms for the remaining supporting questions and their action plan.

Inquiry Graphic Organizer

Compelling Question:
What can I do with my agency?

↓

Hypothesis:

Supporting Question 1:	Supporting Question 2:	Supporting Question 3:	Supporting Question 4:
Are there others like me?	Where do I belong?	What do I see as a need?	What steps are necessary to make change for that need?

Findings:	Findings:	Findings:	Findings:
Revised Hypothesis:	Revised Hypothesis:	Revised Hypothesis:	Revised Hypothesis:

Final Conclusion (should answer CQ and use evidence):

Additional Notes:

Figure 7.1 "What can I do with my agency?" Inquiry Graphic Organizer

Supporting Question 1 Graphic Organizer

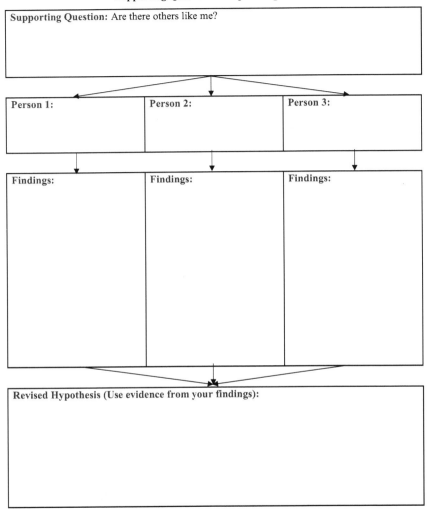

Figure 7.2 "Are there others like me?" Supporting Question 1 Graphic Organizer

Supporting Question 2 Graphic Organizer

Supporting Question: Where do I belong?

Where do I belong at school?	Where do I belong in the community?

Findings:	Findings:

Revised Hypothesis (Use evidence from your findings):

Figure 7.3 "Where do I belong?" Supporting Question 2 Graphic Organizer

Supporting Question 3 Graphic Organizer

Supporting Question: What do I see as a need?

Source: Personal Reflection

Findings:

Revised Hypothesis (Use evidence from your findings):

Figure 7.4 "What do I see as a need?" Supporting Question 3 Graphic Organizer

Supporting Question 4 Graphic Organizer

Supporting Question: What steps are necessary to make change for that need?

Source: Personal Reflection

Findings:

Revised Hypothesis (Use evidence from your findings):

Figure 7.5 "What steps are necessary to make change for that need?" Supporting
Question 4 Graphic Organizer

References

Blevins, B., LeCompte, K., & Wells, S. (2016). Innovations in civic education: Developing civic agency through action civics. *Theory & Research in Social Education, 44*(3), 344–384. https://doi.org/10.1080/00933104.2016.1203853

Hauver, J. (2017). Attending to children's civic learning in the in-between. *Social Studies and the Young Learner, 81*(6), 376–379.

Serriere, S. C. (2005). Empowering young learners with civic agency! *Social Studies and the Young Learner, 17*(4), 1–2.

Silva Dias, T., & Menezes, I. (2014). Children and adolescents as political actors: Collective visions of politics and citizenship. *Journal of Moral Education, 43*(3), 250–268. https://doi.org/10.1080/03057240.2014.918875

8

USING PRIMARY SOURCES

Introduction to Approach

Primary sources are an original object, not a retelling or compilation of other sources. They can include items such as pictures, artifacts, newspaper articles, and journal entries. Using primary sources to teach social studies has long been advocated, mostly in the context of students thinking like historians or doing history through investigations (VanSledright, 2002; Barton & Levstik, 2004). In fact, Barton and Levstik (2004) argue that the goal of using primary sources is to teach with inquiry. They write, "[Inquiry] provides practice in the process of reaching judgments based on evidence, it makes the process of knowledge construction clear, and it may lead to deeper comprehension than transmission-oriented instructional strategies" (p. 202). Students can use primary sources as resources in inquiry in order to start thinking like historians and grapple with competing narratives.

DOI: 10.4324/9781003274148-10

Similar to using children's literature to counter master narratives (see Chapter 6), primary sources can also be used to augment social studies textbooks to lead students to question their prior knowledge. Bickford and O'Farrell (2019) use historical sources to help students question how public figures, such as Eleanor Roosevelt, are taught. They use primary sources so students will learn about her labor movement advocacy, a part of her history often left out of textbooks. Similarly, Bickford et al. (2020) write about fourth graders comparing the work of Martin Luther King Jr. and Frederick Douglass, specifically to make connections between the abolitionist movement, the Civil Rights Movement, and the time period in between. While textbooks have been known to tell one side of history, primary sources, if used correctly, can be used to hear other perspectives.

Primary sources can be integrated into inquiry through doing close readings either at stations or as a whole class. Students can address supporting questions that relate to primary sources, compare different perspectives, or compare primary and secondary sources. While the example provided only uses primary sources in the centers, a mix of primary and secondary sources could also be used. Secondary sources are used in the activating background knowledge portion of the lesson to help students familiarize themselves with the topic.

The lesson described here focuses on the women's suffrage movement, particularly on the art created by suffragists and used during protests and marches. By delving into sources such as music, poetry, banners, and posters/postcards, students view different perspectives from within the suffrage movement. This example also shows types of questions teachers can ask about primary sources. Unlike many other examples in this book, in this lesson, we provide multiple guiding questions in addition to the supporting question at each station. The additional questions help students analyze the source more closely and focus their attention on aspects that might otherwise be overlooked. This becomes less necessary as students gain experience with primary sources, but when students first encounter these types of resources, they may need the extra scaffolding.

When teaching with primary sources, it's also important to consider the context/reading level of your primary source. While some (Wineburg & Martin, 2009) advocate for adapting primary sources to make them easier for students to read, we do not feel that this is necessary for this particular set of sources. The sources provided for this inquiry are music, art, and poetry and to adapt them would be to significantly change the content. In this case, we carefully selected pieces that would be accessible for elementary students. For other inquiries, you should use your discretion about how much can (and should) be adapted for your class use. Frequently, typed transcripts and simplified versions of commonly used primary source documents are available online. If you decide to use alternative versions with your students, we suggest that you pair them with the original when presenting them to students.

The other main consideration when teaching with primary sources is to make sure that you are helping students to make their own interpretations and, in some cases, to make their own questions. Whenever teachers introduce primary sources, they should give students time to evaluate them and to ask questions. Though we do not use primary source analysis worksheets in this lesson, teachers might consider using them for additional scaffolding. We often use the worksheets available at the National Archives website: www.archives.gov/education/lessons/worksheets. These worksheets are tailored to specific types of primary sources such as a photograph or political cartoons, are available in English and Spanish, and have versions for primary and secondary students. Teachers who are unfamiliar with source analysis might also find them helpful as they design and prepare for instruction. The worksheets can be especially helpful in requiring students to give the sources more than a cursory glance.

Content Knowledge

Next is a list of places where teachers can access primary sources:

1. **Library of Congress, www.loc.gov/**
   The Library of Congress has many resources for teachers. Their website is easily accessible and searchable.
2. **National Archives, www.archives.gov/**
   The National Archives also has many resources for teachers, including information on how to teach with primary sources. Their website is also easily accessible and searchable.

3. **Local historical societies**

   Local historical societies are especially helpful when teaching state or local history in younger grades. They usually have access to unique resources and artifacts.

4. **Local libraries**

   Local libraries are also especially helpful for local history teachers. They often have sources that are pertinent to the local area.

Next is a list of resources for the specific topic addressed in this lesson:

1. **Creativity and persistence: Art that fueled the fight for women's suffrage: Published by National Endowment for the Arts, www.arts. gov/sites/default/files/Creativity-and-Persistence-08.13.20.pdf**

   This report is a fantastic resource describing how art was used in the American women's suffrage movement. It also includes numerous examples to include in the classroom.

2. **How the Vote was Won, www.thesuffragettes.org/**

   This site has a wealth of information. It includes background information as well as arts-based primary sources, such as song lyrics and plays. Note: This site focuses on the British movement.

3. **Poetry and the Women's Suffrage Movement, https://poets.org/ text/poetry-and-womens-suffrage-movement**

   This section of a larger poetry site includes some background knowledge and several poems you can page through.

4. **London School of Economics and Political Science Library Artifact photos, www.flickr.com/people/lselibrary/**

   The LSE Library has digitized many documents, banners, buttons, and so on. Look through the albums to find more examples of women's suffrage art. Also, a pamphlet by Lowndes, a famous English banner artist in the movement, can be found here. Note: This is a great site for teachers, but some content may be inappropriate for students, so don't send them here to explore.

5. **Everything You Need to Know about Mary Lowndes, https:// artsandculture.google.com/story/everything-you-need-to-know-about-mary-lowndes/ZgLSVZwiPHTMJA**

This Google story describes how Lowndes shifted from stained glass to banner art. It includes background information, pictures, and references to the guidance she gave other banner makers.

6. **Symbols of the Women's Suffrage Movement, www.nps.gov/ articles/symbols-of-the-women-s-suffrage-movement.htm**
   This site recognizes and explains some commonly found symbols of the suffrage movement.

7. **Woman and Her Sphere, Suffrage Stories: "Silk, Satin, and Suffrage" and Digital Drama's "100 Banners' Project," https:// womanandhersphere.com/tag/suffrage-banners/**
   This article gives great information about the banners and includes pictures of several.

8. **Museum of London's Online Exhibits, https://artsandculture. google.com/partner/museum-of-london**
   Several online exhibits discuss the British women's suffrage movement. These exhibits include background information and photographs of primary sources.

9. **Document Analysis Worksheets, www.archives.gov/education/ lessons/worksheets**
   The National Archives has produced a set of worksheets to support students when analyzing primary sources. These worksheets can supplement this lesson plan or be used in future lessons, and there are Spanish versions available.

Resources for Students

Many of the previous resources can also be used for students. Additionally, here is a list of several children's books about the women's suffrage movement.

1. *Finish the Fight!: The Brave and Revolutionary Women Who Fought for the Right to Vote* **by Veronica Chambers and the staff of** *The New York Times*
   This book gives biographies for 11 different suffrage leaders, focusing on women of color and queer women.

2. **Lifting as We Climb: Black Women's Battle for the Ballot Box by Evette Dionne**

   This book discusses the African American women who fought for suffrage. Often overlooked in the history of the suffrage movement because of the segregation of the movement, this book focuses on women such as Ida B. Wells and Mary Church Terrell.

3. *Around America to Win the Vote: Two Suffragists, a Kitten, and 10,000 Miles* **by Mara Rockliff**

   This picture book tells the story of Nell Richardson and Alice Burke on a trip across the United States in 1916 to support the suffrage movement.

4. **Suffragette: The Battle for Equality by David Roberts**

   This book traces the history of the suffragette movement in both the United Kingdom and the United States.

5. *Equality's Call: The Story of Voting Rights in America* **by Deborah Diesen**

   This book isn't just about the women's suffrage movement but all voting rights movements within the United States.

6. *Mary Church Terrell: Leader for Equality (Revised Edition)* **by Patricia and Fredrick McKissack**

   This is a biography of Mary Church Terrell, an African American leader in the suffrage movement.

7. **Marching with Aunt Susan by Claire Rudolf Murphy**

   This is a book about a young girl who hears Susan B. Anthony speak and begins to fight for women's suffrage. It is based on a true story.

Pedagogy

Compelling Question: How did art contribute to women winning the right to vote?

Objectives:

- Students will be able to analyze primary sources from the women's suffrage movement to determine how art was used within the movement.

Throughout the lesson, we will reference graphic organizers. The "Inquiry Graphic Organizer" synthesizes the full lesson. It will be used at the beginning of the lesson for the compelling question and initial hypothesis. Then students will return to the Inquiry Graphic Organizer each time they complete a supporting question to record their findings and revised hypothesis. It will also be used when they write their final conclusion. The other graphic organizers, "Supporting Question __ Graphic Organizer," will support student inquiry for each of the supporting questions. As they investigate each question, students will complete the appropriate graphic organizer to record their findings for each source and their revised hypothesis. We find it helpful to fill in parts of each graphic organizer with the questions and sources before giving them to students. The graphic organizers for this lesson are provided at the end of the chapter.

Introduction

Activating Background Knowledge

As a class, view the following video about the women's suffrage movement: https://youtu.be/a9LmBgY-F5A

Give students biographies of several of the leaders of the women's suffrage movement. Biographies can be found at www.womenshistory.org/celebrating-centennial/suffragist-biographies and www.brandywine.org/museum/hidden-figures-suffrage-movement.

While viewing the video and investigating the two websites, ask students to define suffrage. Afterwards, discuss suffrage and the movement in general. Some questions might include the following:

- How did the women work for suffrage?
- Who was involved in the women's suffrage movement?
- What was the point of the women's suffrage movement?
- How did individuals impact the suffrage movement?
- What were some conflicts within the suffrage movement? (Be sure to consider the issues of race and class throughout the movement.)

By the end of this discussion, be sure students understand the purpose of the movement, that there were many women involved from all races and socioeconomic statuses, that it took about 80 years to win suffrage, and that there were a variety of methods and tactics used in the fight for women's right to vote.

Note: This inquiry is presented as centers for small groups to complete. The centers may be completed in any order; each will take approximately 15 minutes to complete. It is possible that students could also complete these as a whole class, guided by the teacher.

Introduce Compelling Question

At this point in the lesson, don't discuss the compelling question much. Introduce the question "How did art contribute to women winning the right to vote?" and remind students that the goal for this lesson is to answer this question. Give them the Inquiry Graphic Organizer to write the compelling question. Invite them to silently consider the question for a minute or two. Remind them to think about what they already know that might help them to answer this question.

Hypothesis

After thinking about the compelling question, have students write their initial hypothesis on their graphic organizer. Remind them that it is always good to provide evidence about their thinking but also to remember that this is their initial hypothesis, so it might be a guess at this point. As they continue in the lesson, they will gather more evidence to support their thinking. We recommend that students keep the Inquiry Graphic Organizer at their desk. After completing each station, ask students to return to their desk and revise their hypothesis on the Inquiry Graphic Organizer.

Instructional Procedures

For this lesson, we created a center to address each supporting question that older students can complete independently. We listed the supporting questions and sources here but included the student instructions and lesson materials at the end of the chapter.

Supporting Question 1: How did the suffrage movement use music to promote its cause?
Source:

1. "The March of the Women" by Ethel Smyth
2. "Suffrage Song" by Eleanor Smith
3. "She's Good Enough to be Your Baby's Mother and She's Good Enough to Vote with You" by Alfred Bryan and Herman Paley
4. "Federation Song" by Susie I. Lankford Shorter

Supporting Question 2: What can poetry tell us about the women's suffrage movement?
Source:

1. "Song for Equal Suffrage"
2. "To Susan B. Anthony on her Eightieth Birthday" by Elizabeth Cady Stanton
3. "Aunt Chloe's Politics" by Frances Ellen Watkins Harper

Supporting Question 3: How were banners used in the suffrage movement, and what contributions did they make?
Source:

1. Picture of banner, which says: We were voters out west! Why deny our rights in the East
2. Picture of banners that say: We demand an amendment to the United States Constitution Enfranchising Women and Welcome Suffrage Envoys
3. Picture of banners that say: Mr. President how long must women wait for liberty and Mr. President what will you do for woman suffrage
4. Picture of banner that says: Banner State Women's National Baptist Convention
5. Pictures of banner that says: Mr. President what will you do for woman suffrage in a museum and outside of the White House

6. Picture of banner that says: Lifting as We Climb
7. Picture of banner that says: Federation of Colored Women 1910

Supporting Question 3: How did members of the women's suffrage movement use posters and/or postcards to encourage laws to be changed?
Source:

1. Picture of a poster that has a picture of two children. It reads:
   VOTES FOR WOMEN
   For the work, For the taxes we pay, For the Laws we obey, We want something to say.
2. Picture of a poster that has a picture of four babies, including one holding a sign reading VOTES FOUR OUR MOTHERS. The rest of the poster reads:

GIVE MOTHER THE VOTE
   WE NEED IT
   OUR FOOD OUR HEALTH OUR PLAY OUR HOMES OUR SCHOOLS
OUR WORK ARE RULED BY MEN'S VOTES
   Isn't it a funny thing that Father cannot see Why Mother ought to have a vote on how these things should be? THINK IT OVER

Conclusion

When everyone has completed all four centers, invite them back to revise their hypothesis of the compelling question one more time. Explain to them that this will be their conclusion, or final answer, for the compelling question. Also, remind them to reference their supporting questions and evidence from the four centers. It might be helpful to model how to use evidence from their centers as support for their final conclusion, especially if this is one of the first times students are using primary sources within their inquiry to answer the compelling question. This can also be modeled after each center so students practice explaining their arguments using information from the primary sources.

Optional Extension

After students have completed the inquiry about how art and music was used for the suffrage movement, they may be able to make connections with art used in current social or civil rights movements. They may also wish to create their own art for a current issue.

Adaptability and Differentiation

Early Childhood

This lesson is already well-suited for early childhood classrooms. Students can listen to the songs or have the poems read to them. The banners and postcards can also be read to them as they look at the images. Some of the guiding questions within the stations might need to be adjusted for this age level. Instead of completing the centers independently, young students should be guided through each center with their teacher. The analysis of primary sources can also occur as a whole class, at least at first.

Middle Level

This lesson can be a starting point for middle-level students to look deeper into women's suffrage. They can spend more time researching the women mentioned in the biographies in the introduction to the lesson. They also can create their own questions and research other art used during the suffrage movement.

Students with Special Needs

It would be helpful to have image descriptions for each of the images provided as well as using the sound recordings of the songs or of the poems being read. It may also be a good idea to complete the centers as a whole class or within small groups.

Inquiry Graphic Organizer

Compelling Question:	
How did art contribute to women winning the right to vote?	

↓

Hypothesis:

Supporting Question 1:	**Supporting Question 2:**	**Supporting Question 3:**	**Supporting Question 4:**
How did the suffrage movement use music to promote its cause?	What can poetry tell us about the women's suffrage movement?	How were banners used in the Suffrage movement and what contributions did they make?	How did members of the women's suffrage movement use posters and/or postcards to encourage laws to be changed?

Findings:	**Findings:**	**Findings:**	**Findings:**
Revised Hypothesis:	**Revised Hypothesis:**	**Revised Hypothesis:**	**Revised Hypothesis:**

Final Conclusion (should answer CQ and use evidence):

Additional Notes:

Figure 8.1 "How did art contribute to women winning the right to vote?" Inquiry Graphic Organizer

Supporting Question 1 Graphic Organizer

Supporting Question: How did the suffrage movement use music to promote its cause?			
Source 1: "The March of the Women" by Ethel Smyth	**Source 2:** "Suffrage Song" by Eleanor Smith	**Source 3:** "She's Good Enough to be your Baby's Mother and She's Good Enough to Vote with You" by Alfred Bryan and Herman Paley	**Source 4:** "Federation Song" by Susie I. Lankford Shorter
Findings:	**Findings:**	**Findings:**	**Findings:**
Revised Hypothesis (Use evidence from your findings):			

Figure 8.2 "How did the suffrage movement use music to promote its cause?" Supporting Question 1 Graphic Organizer

Supporting Question 2 Graphic Organizer

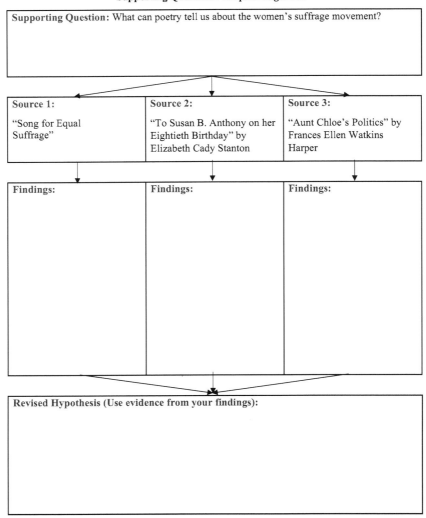

Figure 8.3 "What can poetry tell us about the women's suffrage movement?" Supporting Question 2 Graphic Organizer

Supporting Question 3 Graphic Organizer

Supporting Question: How were banners used in the Suffrage movement and what contributions did they make?

Source: Women's Suffrage Banner Photographs

Findings:

Revised Hypothesis (Use evidence from your findings):

Figure 8.4 "How were banners used in the Suffrage movement and what contributions did they make?" Supporting Question 3 Graphic Organizer

Supporting Question 4 Graphic Organizer

Supporting Question: How did members of the women's suffrage movement use posters and/or postcards to encourage laws to be changed?

Source 1: Poster reading "VOTES FOR WOMEN For the work, For the taxes we pay, For the Laws we obey, We want something to say"	Source 2: Poster reading "VOTES FOUR OUR MOTHERS. GIVE MOTHER THE VOTE WE NEED IT OUR FOOD OUR HEALTH OUR PLAY OUR HOMES OUR SCHOOLS OUR WORK ARE RULED BY MEN'S VOTES Isn't it a funny thing that Father cannot see Why Mother ought to have a vote on how these things should be? THINK IT OVER

Findings:	Findings:

Revised Hypothesis (Use evidence from your findings):

Figure 8.5 "How did members of the women's suffrage movement use posters and/or postcards to encourage laws to be changed?" Supporting Question 4 Graphic Organizer

References

Barton, K. C., & Levstik, L. S. (2004). *Teaching history for the common good.* Routledge.

Bickford, J. H., Clabough, J., & Taylor, T. (2020). Fourth graders' (re-)reading (historical) thinking, and (revised) writing about the black freedom movement. *The Journal of Social Studies Research, 44*(2) 249–261. https://doi.org/10.1016/j.jssr.2020.01.001

Bickford, J. H., & O'Farrell, B. (2019). Exploring Eleanor Roosevelt's labor advocacy using primary and secondary sources. *Social Studies Research and Practice, 14*(1), 64–77.

VanSledright, B. (2002). *In search of America's past: Learning to read history in elementary school.* Teachers College Press.

Wineburg, S., & Martin, D. (2009). Tampering with history: Adapting primary sources for struggling readers. *Social Education, 73*(5), 212–216.

Music Center

In this center, students will listen to performances and/or read the lyrics of various songs and marches that were used during the suffrage movement. They will compare and contrast each of the songs and determine the authors' purposes.

Supporting Question: How did the suffrage movement use music to promote its cause?

Student Directions:

Music was used throughout the women's suffrage movement for many different reasons. Sometimes the songs were *anthems* meant to uplift a group of people. Other times they were *marches* with strong beats to guide a parade. They even used *popular songs* and changed the lyrics to match their cause.

Today, you are going to listen to three songs and read the lyrics, or words, for those plus one more.

After each song, answer the following questions:

1. What did you notice when listening to this song?
2. How did it make you feel?
3. Read the lyrics. Did you know that not everyone wanted women to have the right to vote? Because women were not allowed to vote, only men could make a new law to give them suffrage. Do you think this song would be effective to persuade men to give women the right to vote?
4. Write down one quote from the song that might persuade others.

Now answer the supporting question. Finally, revisit your hypothesis for the compelling question.

March: "The March of the Women" by Ethel Smyth

Listen to the song: https://youtu.be/KKp2r8_P5Do

Image: www.exploringsurreyspast.org.uk/collections/getrecord/SHCOL_
     9180_9_5

Lyrics: www.protestsonglyrics.net/Women_Feminism_Songs/March-of-
     the-Women.phtml

Anthem: "Suffrage Song" by Eleanor Smith

Listen to the song: https://youtu.be/1BGLsYnQfRY
Image: https://hdl.loc.gov/loc.music/mussuffrage.mussuffrage-100060
Lyrics: www.protestsonglyrics.net/Women_Feminism_Songs/Suffrage-
    Song.phtml

Popular Song: "She's Good Enough to be Your Baby's Mother and She's Good Enough to Vote with You" by Alfred Bryan and Herman Paley

Listen to the song: www.youtube.com/watch?v=HxF_afsWnZQ
Image: https://hdl.loc.gov/loc.music/mussuffrage.mussuffrage-100123
Lyrics: https://lewissuffragecollection.omeka.net/items/show/1306

Federation Song: "Federation Song" by Susie I. Lankford Shorter

This song, sung to the tune of *Glory, Glory Hallelujah*, was sung at national
    meetings of the National Association of Colored Women's Clubs.
Pictured: Club pin depicting the motto for the National Association of
    Colored Women's Clubs found at: https://bit.ly/3o5I4q6
Lyrics: https://bit.ly/3rjW3up

Poetry Center

At this center, the students will read poetry that was frequently published in women's newspapers and analyze it for common themes.

Supporting Question: What can poetry tell us about the women's suffrage movement?

Student Directions:

Poetry was used throughout the women's suffrage movement. Suffragists frequently had their poems published in newspapers that supported suffrage. At this center, you will read through three different poems written about suffrage and answer the following questions about each poem:

1. What images/symbols stand out to you in this poem?
2. What do you think the theme or message is?
3. What do you think the mood of the poem is?
4. Why do you think this poem was written?

After answering the questions for each poem, answer the supporting question. Finally, revisit your hypothesis to the compelling question.

Poem 1: "Song for Equal Suffrage" by Charlotte Perkins Gilman

Link: https://poets.org/poem/song-equal-suffrage

**Poem 2: "To Susan B. Anthony on her Eightieth Birthday"
by Elizabeth Cady Stanton**

Link: https://poets.org/text/poetry-and-womens-suffrage-movement
This poem was written from one of the founding mothers of the suffrage
    movement to another founding mother. Neither lived to see the
    Nineteenth Amendment passed.

Poem 3: "Aunt Chloe's Politics" by Frances Ellen Watkins Harper

Link: https://poets.org/poem/aunt-chloes-politics

Banner Center

In this center, students will look at the banners that marchers carried during the movement. They will examine banners made and used in both the US and England.

Supporting questions:

• How were banners used in the suffrage movement, and what contributions did they make?

Student Directions:

Banners were used throughout the women's suffrage movement. Suffragists frequently made banners to represent their group or town in a parade. They also used banners to display their messages. At this center, you will look at banners from the United States.

For each of the banners, answer the following questions:

1. What do you notice first?
2. What catches your eye?
3. Why do you think these banners were made?
4. How were they used?
5. Who used them?

When you have analyzed each of the banners, answer the supporting question for this station. Then revisit your hypothesis for the compelling question.

1. Picture of banner, which says: We were voters out west! Why deny our rights in the East
   Link: Photo: https://womanssuffrageyay.weebly.com/i-objective-conditions.html
   This picture was taken in Toronto, Ontario, Canada.*
2. Picture of banners that say: We demand an amendment to the United States Constitution Enfranchising Women and Welcome Suffrage Envoys
   Link: https://thesuffieldobserver.com/2019/10/the-19th-amendment

3. Picture of banners that say: Mr. President how long must women wait for liberty and Mr. President what will you do for woman suffrage
Link: www.loc.gov/pictures/item/97500299/

4. Picture of Banner that says: Banner State Women's National Baptist Convention
Link: https://lccn.loc.gov/93505051

5. Pictures of banner that says: Mr. President what will you do for woman suffrage in a museum and outside of the White House
Museum link: https://s.si.edu/3G0MqEX
White House link: www.loc.gov/pictures/item/97500299/

6. Picture of banner that says: Lifting as We Climb
Link: https://s.si.edu/3HzPg5h

7. Picture of Banner that says: Federation of Colored Women 1910
Link: https://s.si.edu/3Hwy6pj

Poster and Postcard Center

In this center, students will look at several different types of posters that were used to promote their cause at marches and other public events. Postcards, along with posters, were also used to endorse suffrage through mailing or posting them for others to see.

Supporting Question:

How did members of the women's suffrage movement use posters and/ or postcards to encourage laws to be changed?

Student Directions:

Posters and postcards were used in the women's suffrage movement to draw attention to why women should have the right to vote. Look at the two provided. Compare and contrast them.

1. Do they catch your attention?
2. What do you notice first?
3. What similar themes are on the two posters?
4. What symbols or images do you see?
5. What message do they send?
6. Are these effective at promoting women's right to vote?

Then answer the supporting question and revisit your hypothesis for the compelling question.

Postcard and poster link:

www.arts.gov/sites/default/files/Creativity-and-Persistence-08.13.20.pdf

9

EVALUATING SOURCES

Introduction to Approach

Each type of source merits evaluation and online sources, especially, need to be evaluated for credibility. The Stanford History Education Group (SHEG) looked at how individuals with PhDs in history, fact-checkers, and college students evaluated online information and found that those with history PhDs and college students could be easily duped by false information but that fact-checkers had an advantage (Wineburg & McGrew, 2017). The key difference in the fact-checker's approach was lateral reading or reading across multiple sources to verify the information's accuracy. This research indicates that the strategies used to evaluate sources are important. Not all methods and strategies will be able to evaluate source credibility equally.

We contend that using source evaluation as a part of inquiry learning teaches students how to fact-check and judge credibility in an authentic way. Although this lesson is designed to teach source evaluation, we encourage teachers to make it a part of each inquiry or anytime they

DOI: 10.4324/9781003274148-11

use an online source with students in order for the students to realize its importance and adopt the practice independently. It is also important to note that source evaluation cannot really be pared down to a specific strategy or test (Tardiff, 2020). Narrowing down source evaluation to a checklist or particular strategy might prevent the reader from visiting other sources, which is a key strategy of information literacy. Instead, it is suggested that teachers and students develop several skills that can be used when appropriate to the source and context. In the next section, we outline a few key skills and strategies that both teachers and students can use when evaluating sources.

Lateral Reading

As noted earlier, lateral reading is one of the key strategies for source evaluation (Wineburg & McGrew, 2017). Put simply, lateral reading is reading other sources to verify information. Online, it usually means opening a second web page and searching to confirm the accuracy of the initial page. For example, lateral reading might entail a quick internet search to check if other sites corroborate a fact. It might also mean checking an author's credentials through another source or looking further into the publisher's worldview on their about page.

Lateral reading is arguably the most important skill in information literacy. We highly encourage you and your students to always look for corroboration of facts and information from other sources. However, there are additional strategies that are helpful in guiding the types of information the reader might look for.

CCOW

CCOW is an acronym to guide source evaluation (Tardiff, 2020). It is not all-encompassing, but it reminds the reader to look at some important factors in source evaluation and requires lateral reading. Here is a brief outline of the factors:

Credentials: Who is the author? If you can't find one, that is not a good sign. Is the author an expert on this topic? An internet search of the author's name should pull up enough information to verify their expertise. But be sure they are knowledgeable about the topic at hand. An expert in history, for example, may not be able to speak about a new scientific discovery. Also, investigate the publishing organization. This can start on the "About" page of the website, but it is good practice to search for the organization too.

Claims: Is the information on the site current, accurate, and cited? Consider the topic to determine if the information is up to date. An article on COVID-19 from early 2020 is likely to be too old to be helpful. However, an article on the Wright brothers' first flight from 2020 is likely to contain up-to-date information. To determine the accuracy of the information, look for corroboration from other experts. Remember to check those experts' credentials too. If you find a general consensus, then it is likely to be factual. Also, look to see if the information is cited and if those citations are reliable too. Follow the links to examine the other websites and information cited. Is it also accurate and reliable? Written by an expert? If there are no citations, that is likely a red flag.

Objectives: Why was this piece created? Is it news? Satire? A sales pitch? Part of a political campaign? Understanding why a text was created is important because the purpose should influence your reading. For example, if you read an article about the benefits of eating dairy, the facts might be accurate, but if it was produced by the Dairy Farmers of America and is designed to convince you to buy dairy products, you should keep that in mind as you read. In that case, a scholarly article by a dietician at a university may provide more useful information about dairy consumption.

Worldview: Both the author and the reader have a worldview shaped by beliefs and life experiences. These worldviews impact the way we present and take in information. Everyone has a worldview; it is unavoidable. But as we read, it is important to examine the worldview of the author and how our own worldview impacts how we take in the information. If you are politically left leaning and read an article from a news outlet with a right-wing perspective, you are more likely to be skeptical of its claims than if you shared a similar worldview. Some might consider worldview to be the same as bias. However, bias carries a negative connotation, which is why we suggest using "worldview" instead. Worldviews (and biases) are unavoidable and, therefore, an important consideration when evaluating sources.

Web Domain

Many of us have been told to pay attention to a site's web domain when evaluating it. Although this may have once been a tried-and-true method, it should not be the only method employed. Oftentimes, people consider information rom .gov, .org, or .edu to be most reliable but that is not always the case. Because most universities have web space available to students, a .edu site, for example, may publish a student project that has factual errors. On the other hand, a .com site might link to scholarly works. The web domain might be a fine starting point, but it is very important to look beyond that and to ensure that is not the depth of student skills.

Fact Checking

Sometimes sources or information is checked by an outside source. Fact-checkers such as Snopes, Politifact, and FactCheck.Org will frequently check the reliability of news or popular media stories. Searching for information along with "fact-check" or visiting a fact-check website and searching there directly will sometimes give you all the information you need.

The lesson plan in this chapter asks students to use several sources to answer their compelling question: "Is safe drinking water a right?" Students begin by evaluating sources to determine their credibility. From there, students use credible sources to answer supporting questions, which focus on the safety of drinking water and how natural disasters impact our water supply.

Content Knowledge

As mentioned earlier, there are various resources and strategies for source evaluation. Here are more resources, which are useful for teaching and learning more.

1. *AdFontes Media,* https://adfontesmedia.com/
    This website was founded to allow individuals to see how media sources stack up in relation to how much of their reporting is fact vs. opinion and if the source tends to lean right or left. The Media

Bias Chart houses much of that data, but the site also includes educator resources. Many resources are available for free, including the media bias chart, but some features require membership.

2. *AllSides,* **www.allsides.com/unbiased-balanced-news**

AllSides' website states, "unbiased news does not exist; we provide balanced news and civil discourse." It can help sift through online material and determine the worldview of a source because it ranks media bias as to if they lean left, right, or center. If you are looking for a particular topic, it places left, right, and center sources and articles side by side so you can easily read balanced coverage.

3. *Factitious,* **http://factitious.augamestudio.com/#/**

This is a fun game that could be played with students at any level or to test your own skills at source evaluation. As you answer questions, it will give you more information about how the source was evaluated.

4. *Stanford Civic Online Reasoning,* **https://cor.stanford.edu/**

This website has numerous resources for teachers, including a full curriculum, videos, and lesson plans to use in the classroom. The "Research" section has links to many of the articles they have written that describe their work for general and scholarly audiences.

5. **Web Literacy for Student Fact-Checkers . . . and other people who care about facts by Mike Caulfield, https://webliteracy. pressbooks.com/**

Although written for students, this open-access eBook is very helpful when learning more about media literacy. It presents several evaluation strategies, and the field guide section at the conclusion of the book presents ways to search and source information.

Pedagogy

Compelling Question: Is safe drinking water a right?

Objectives:

- Students will be able to evaluate sources for credibility.
- Students will be able to explain how to evaluate sources.
- Students will be able to conclude if safe drinking water is a right based on evidence from their inquiry.

Throughout the lesson, we will reference graphic organizers. The "Inquiry Graphic Organizer" synthesizes the full lesson. It will be used at the beginning of the lesson for the compelling question and initial hypothesis. Then students will return to the Inquiry Graphic Organizer each time they complete a supporting question to record their findings and revised hypothesis. It will also be used when they write their final conclusion. The other graphic organizers, "Supporting Question __ Graphic Organizer," will support student inquiry for each of the supporting questions. As they investigate each question, students will complete the appropriate graphic organizer to record their findings for each source and their revised hypothesis. We find it helpful to fill in parts of each graphic organizer with the questions and sources before giving them to students. The graphic organizers for this lesson are provided at the end of the chapter.

Introduction

Activating Background Knowledge

Begin by discussing the importance of water. Ask small groups to create a list of ten reasons water is important to our daily lives.

Next, show students this infographic from the United Nations: www. un.org/waterforlifedecade/pdf/facts_and_figures_human_right_to_ water_eng.pdf.

Read through the infographic as a class. Then allow students another 5–10 minutes to discuss and reflect upon it. Have students revisit the question "Why is water important?" and see if they want to make any changes to their list.

Introduce Compelling Question

At this point in the lesson, don't discuss the compelling question much. Introduce the question "Is safe drinking water a right?" and remind students that the goal for this lesson is to answer this question. Give them the Inquiry Graphic Organizer to write the compelling question. Invite them to silently consider the question for a minute or two. Remind them to think about what they already know that might help them to answer this question.

Hypothesis

After thinking about the compelling question, have students write their initial hypothesis on their graphic organizer. Remind them that it is always good to provide evidence about their thinking but also to remember that this is their initial hypothesis, so it might be a guess at this point. As they continue in the lesson, they will gather more evidence to support their thinking. We recommend that students keep the Inquiry Graphic Organizer at their desk. After completing each station, ask students to return to their desk and revise their hypothesis on the Inquiry Graphic Organizer.

Instructional Procedures

Note: We suggest competing this lesson in two parts: Part 1: Evaluating Sources and Part 2: Inquiry Activity. This will allow the teacher to prepare the Inquiry Graphic Organizers according to how the class sorted the sources. When evaluating sources in our daily lives, we usually evaluate them as we read and engage with them. In a middle-grade classroom, though, we think it is important that the teacher supports the process, and therefore, we have it at the beginning of the lesson. However, in the adaptability and differentiation section, we discuss how teachers might integrate the two processes in a more authentic manner.

Part 1: Evaluating Sources

Explain to students that in order to answer this question, they first need to evaluate which of the sources you provided are credible. Tell them that they are going to evaluate several sources with varying degrees of credibility. It will be their job to evaluate the credibility and piece the evidence together to determine how to answer the compelling question.

At this point in the lesson, students should begin to focus on how to evaluate sources. Introduce the CCOW Questionnaire and walk students through the websites listed in the chart. Remind them that this is just a tool and there are many strategies that they can and should use to evaluate sources.

Table 9.1 CCOW Questionnaire

Source	Credentials: Is the author an expert?	Claims: Is it current, accurate, and cited?	Objectives: Why was this written?	Worldview: What is the author's worldview? How does it relate to mine?	Other evidence/ Notes

Sorting Activity

As you evaluate each site, you will engage in a two-level sorting activity using the CCOW Questionnaire. First, you and the students will decide if it belongs in the group for reliable or unreliable sources based on CCOW or other strategies. Model how to evaluate the first few websites using the CCOW Questionnaire and sorting them accordingly. Then ask students to go through the rest of the sources listed. It may work better for your class to divide students into groups and allow each group to look at one to two sources. When deciding on the sources to use, continue to refer them to the CCOW Questionnaire and ask students for their reasons to use or not use the site. Return to the whole group and discuss which websites they classified as reliable or not. Be sure to ask them why they classified them this way. As a class, try to come to a consensus on each site.

After students have explored the sources, help them determine where each site should be used in the inquiry. This is the second level of the sorting activity. Post the three supporting questions:

1. What causes drinking water to become unsafe?
2. Do we have safe drinking water in the US?
3. How do natural disasters impact our water supply?

Review the sources considered reliable and then discuss which question(s) they might answer. Sort them accordingly on the sorting sheet. These will be the sources reviewed for each question. Before doing this lesson, the teacher should have reviewed the sites and classified them so they

Table 9.2 Sorting Sheet

Reliable Source Name	Supporting Question	Why Does It Fit with Your Chosen Question?
CDC: Preparing a Home Water Supply	3	This CDC site discusses how to ensure you are drinking safe water after a natural disaster.

have an idea where they best fit. At the same time, allow the students to provide their evidence and make their conclusions as independently as possible. Feel free to add some sources that you feel might also be helpful. It is also important to note that the internet, being a dynamic resource, may have website changes. There is a brief description of each site on the Source Guide at the end of the chapter that should help you find something similar if the original site is removed.

Full citations, including web addresses, are included in the bibliography section. We provided a copy of how we sorted the sources on the Source Guide at the conclusion of this chapter.

We suggest stopping the lesson here and beginning the inquiry activity the following day. This will allow you to prepare the graphic organizers based on how the students categorized the sources. There are a lot of charts and graphic organizers in this lesson, so inserting the sorted sources onto the supporting questions graphic organizer will eliminate students having to work with so many different pieces at once. Also, be sure to have each graphic organizer labeled correctly. We are including a copy of the graphic organizers, according to our sort, for each supporting question.

Part 2: Inquiry Activity

After determining which sources should be used to answer each supporting question, introduce the inquiry activity by reminding students of the compelling question: "Is safe drinking water a right?" Explain that students will address three supporting questions but think about the compelling question again after each one. Remind them to continue to evaluate the perspective and/or bias of the sources as they gather evidence. This remainder of this lesson is designed to be completed in small groups at stations.

Each station is set up similarly. Students should do the following:

1. Read the supporting question.
2. Read, explore, and discuss the source(s) with their group to find answers to the question.
3. Record evidence and notes from the source in the appropriate box.
4. Make a conclusion to answer the supporting question based on their evidence.
5. Return to their desk and read the compelling question again. Then revise their hypothesis based on their findings at that station.

Supporting Question 1: What causes drinking water to become unsafe?
Sources:

1. *Centers for Disease Control: Water Contamination and Diseases*
   This website provides information about diseases found in unsanitary water.
2. *National Public Radio: What makes Water Unsafe? Not the Color, Taste or Smell: #WorldWater Day*
   This article provides information about how water can be contaminated but appear normal.
3. *The Groundwater Foundation*
   This website gives some basics about where our water comes from as well as some potential threats to water quality.

Supporting Question 2: Do we have safe drinking water in the US?
Sources:

1. *Environmental Protection Agency: Healthy Schools Healthy Kids (January 2017)*
   This EPA website from January 2017 describes healthy schools and the air and water quality throughout the United States. Although the site is in archives, it continues to provide useful information at an accessible level.

2. *The New York Times: "Here are the Places that Struggle to Meet the Rules on Safe Drinking Water"*
   This news article provides information about parts of the US where water quality has deteriorated.
3. *NBC News: "Lead in Water: Study shows many schools have far too much"*
   This news article provides information from a study about lead in schools' water supplies.

Supporting Question 3: How do natural disasters impact our water supply?
Source:

1. *DrinkTap: Water Emergencies*
   This site is produced by the American Water Works Association, which is dedicated to clean water. This page outlines how people can ensure they have safe water after a disaster.
2. *The Center for Watershed Protection: The Impact of Wildfires on Water*
   This article outlines how wildfires impact the water supply.
3. *The New York Times: "Tonga's Airport is Finally Cleared, but Ash Still Poses a Range of Threats"*
   This article describes the impact on a volcanic eruption on the local air and water quality in Tonga.
4. *Centers for Disease Control: Preparing a Home Water Supply*
   This CDC site discusses how to ensure you are drinking safe water after a natural disaster.

Conclusion

After completing each supporting question, bring the students together for a whole class discussion. Be sure to discuss the supporting and compelling questions, as well as the credibility of their findings. You might ask questions such as the following: What makes you think access to drinking water is or is not a right? How did the credible sources help you answer the question? Do you think your answer would have changed if you had used non-credible sources? Why or why not?

Optional Extension

This inquiry lends itself well to an extension involving civic action. After students have discussed the questions in the previous section, ask: "What types of action can we take as a class?" Try to allow the project to be as student-driven as possible. Ask them what they think the biggest needs are, both locally and elsewhere. Then explore ways they might have influence. Here are some ideas:

- Write local officials or school board members to have local water tested for lead.
- Join the citizen science grant through Virginia Tech and test the water in their homes or school.
- Create or join a campaign for fresh drinking water abroad.
- Design a school-wide PSA campaign about the necessity of clean drinking water.
- Trace the source of local water. Host a cleanup day for the local water source, if possible.

Adaptability and Differentiation

Early Childhood

At this level, conducting the inquiry as a whole class is helpful so the teacher can provide ample scaffolding. Students in the early grades should start with discussing the need for clean drinking water in order to survive. After that, we would suggest including a few sources to evaluate, but the teacher will need to heavily scaffold this activity. For example, they might highlight a few statements that are strong evidence of reliability and ask students if they think those statements sound true and why. Another example would be to talk about businesses trying to sell something to consumers and if that makes their goal to present the best information or to present information that makes the consumer want to buy their product. Additionally, several of the cited sources will be too complex for young readers. Several of them may be able to have excerpts used with the students, and we suggest supplementing with videos and visual media, such as infographics on drinking water safety.

Middle School

This lesson can be used with middle school students as-is. However, you may want to include more sources. Another idea would be to include additional sources that focus on the scientific aspects of this question. We suggest including an additional supporting question such as the following: "What are some of the most common chemical pollutants of water?" "How does drinking water impact the area wildlife?" or "Do filtration systems work with contaminated water?"

Middle school would also be a great place to integrate the processes of source evaluation and inquiry. To do this, we suggest giving the students all of the sources or simply giving them the questions and having them find their own sources. As they review the sources, they should use CCOW or other strategies to determine their credibility before using them as evidence. Give them permission to "throw out" sources that they consider unreliable but have them explain why they evaluated them that way.

Differentiation for Student Needs

There is a plethora of resources online at various reading levels that can support differing student needs. Also, grouping students in mixed-ability groups might work well for this lesson. Teachers can also support students with other types of sources, such as videos or visual aids, that might aid students who struggle with the original sources.

Inquiry Graphic Organizer

Compelling Question: Is safe drinking water a right?		

Hypothesis:		

| **Supporting Question 1:**

 What causes drinking water to become unsafe? | **Supporting Question 2:**

Do we have safe drinking water in the US? | **Supporting Question 3:**

How do natural disasters impact our water supply? |

Findings:	**Findings:**	**Findings:**
Revised Hypothesis:	**Revised Hypothesis:**	**Revised Hypothesis:**

Final Conclusion (should answer CQ and use evidence):

Additional Notes:

Figure 9.1 "Is safe drinking water a right?" Inquiry Graphic Organizer

Supporting Question 1 Graphic Organizer

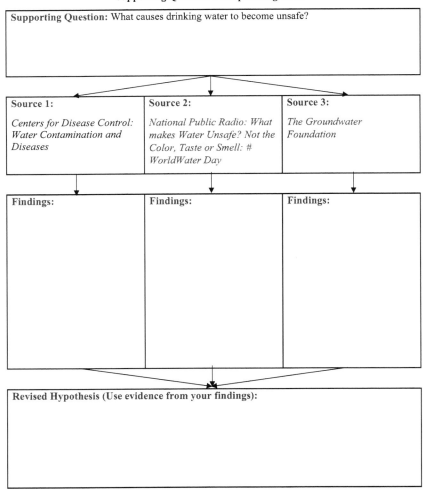

Figure 9.2 "What causes drinking water to become unsafe?" Supporting Question 1 Graphic Organizer

Supporting Question 2 Graphic Organizer

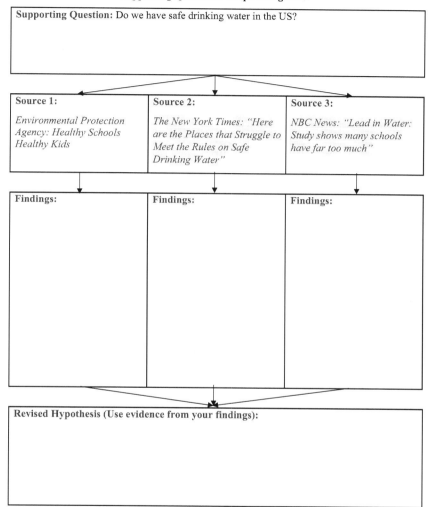

Supporting Question: Do we have safe drinking water in the US?

Source 1:

Environmental Protection Agency: Healthy Schools Healthy Kids

Source 2:

The New York Times: "Here are the Places that Struggle to Meet the Rules on Safe Drinking Water"

Source 3:

NBC News: "Lead in Water: Study shows many schools have far too much"

Findings:

Findings:

Findings:

Revised Hypothesis (Use evidence from your findings):

Figure 9.3 "Do we have safe drinking water in the US?" Supporting Question 2 Graphic Organizer

Supporting Question 3 Graphic Organizer

Supporting Question: How do natural disasters impact our water supply?			
Source 1: DrinkTap: Water Emergencies	**Source 2:** The Center for Watershed Protection: The Impact of Wildfires on Water	**Source 3:** The New York Times: "Tonga's Airport is Finally Cleared, but Ash Still Poses a Range of Threats	**Source 4:** Centers for Disease Control: Preparing a Home Water Supply
Findings:	**Findings:**	**Findings:**	**Findings:**

Revised Hypothesis (Use evidence from your findings):

Figure 9.4 "How do natural disasters impact our water supply?" Supporting
Question 3 Graphic Organizer

Table 9.3 Source Guide

Source Name	Reliable (Y/N)	Supporting Question	Description
CDC: Preparing a Home Water Supply	Y	3	This CDC site discusses how to ensure you are drinking safe water after a natural disaster.
Culligan: Natural Disasters and Drinking Water: How to Keep Your Family Safe	N		Although this website has some helpful information about how to handle water safety after a disaster, it is designed to sell water filters.
EPA: Healthy Schools Healthy Kids (January 2017)	Y	2	This EPA website from January 2017 describes healthy schools and the air and water quality throughout the United States.
CDC: Water Contamination and Diseases	Y	1	This website provides information about diseases found in unsanitary water.
TAPP Water	N		This website recommends buying a filter for US tap water because it is not safe enough to drink.
NY Times: Here Are the Places That Struggle to Meet the Rules on Safe Drinking Water.	Y	2	This news article from February 2018 provides information about parts of the US where water quality has deteriorated.
NPR: What Makes Water Unsafe? Not The Color, Taste Or Smell: #WorldWaterDay	Y	1	This article provides information about how water can be contaminated but appear normal.
The Groundwater Foundation	Y	1	This website gives some basics about where our water comes from as well as some potential threats to water quality.
NBC News: Lead in water: Study shows many schools have far too much	Y	2	This news article from January 2019 provides information from a recent study about lead in schools' water supplies.
Food Revolution	N		This website claims that there are cancer-causing chemicals in 75% of US tap water.
Water Emergencies	Y	3	This site is produced by the American Water Works Association, which is dedicated to clean water. This page outlines how people can ensure they have safe water after a disaster.
Aquasana	N		This website explains why tap water could be unsafe and then encourages readers to buy a water filter.
Center for Watershed Protection: The Impact of Wildfires on Water	Y	3	This article outlines how wildfires impact the water supply.
NY Times: Tonga's Airport Is Finally Cleared, but Ash Still Poses a Range of Threats	Y	3	This article describes the impact on a volcanic eruption on the local air and water quality in Tonga.

Bibliography

American Water Works Association. (n.d.). Water emergencies. *DrinkTap*. Retrieved October 9, 2022, from https://drinktap.org/Water-Info/Questions-About-Water/Water-Emergencies

Brink, S. (2016, March 22). What makes water unsafe? Not the color, taste or smell: #WorldWaterDay. *NPR*. www.npr.org/sections/goatsandsoda/2016/03/22/471408630/what-makes-water-unsafe-not-the-color-taste-or-smell-worldwaterday

Centers for Disease Control. (2021, May 17). Preparing a home water supply. *Water Sanitation, & Hygiene (WASH)-Related Emergencies & Outbreaks*. www.cdc.gov/healthywater/emergency/preparing-a-home-water-supply.html

Centers for Disease Control. (2022, May 26). Water contamination and diseases. *Healthy Water*. www.cdc.gov/healthywater/drinking/contamination.html

Culligan Water. (n.d.). *Natural disasters and drinking water: How to keep your family safe*. Retrieved October 9, 2022, from www.culligannation.com/natural-disasters-drinking-water

Fox, M. (2019, January 9). Lead in water: Study shows many schools have far too much. *NBC News*. www.nbcnews.com/health/health-news/lead-water-study-shows-many-schools-have-far-too-much-n956851

Groundwater Foundation. (n.d.). *Groundwater basics*. Retrieved October 9, 2022, from www.groundwater.org/get-informed/basics/basics.html

Ives, M., & Nagourney, E. (2022, January 20). Tonga's airport is finally cleared, but Ash still poses a range of threats. *The New York Times*. www.nytimes.com/2022/01/20/world/asia/tonga-eruption-ash.html

Maxson, R. (2019, June 19). *The impact of wildfires on water*. Center for Watershed Protection. https://cwp.org/the-impact-of-wildfires-on-water/

Plumer, B., & Popovich, N. (2018, February 12). Here are the places that struggle to meet the rules on safe drinking water. *The New York Times*. Retrieved October 9, 2022, from www.nytimes.com/2018/02/12/climate/drinking-water-safety.html

Tardiff, A. (2020). Have a CCOW. *Foley Library*. https://researchguides.gonzaga.edu/CCOW/start

United States Environmental Protection Agency. (n.d.). *Schools: Air and water quality* [Collections and lists]. Retrieved October 9, 2022, from https://19january2017snapshot.epa.gov/schools-air-water-quality

Wineburg, S., & Mcgrew, S. (2017). *Lateral reading: Reading less and learning more when evaluating digital information* (Stanford History Education Group Working Paper No. 2017-A1). SSRN. https://ssrn.com/abstract=3048994 or http://dx.doi.org/10.2139/ssrn.3048994

10

FOCUSING ON GLOBAL ISSUES

Introduction to Approach

Global citizenship has long been important and will continue to be a critical role of our students. In approaching global issues, we must consider events or issues within the context of a particular time, place, and culture, as well as their impact on the local and global population. In this section, we will outline a few guidelines and suggestions for using inquiry to teach global issues and events in the classroom. Because of potentially controversial topics, difficult discussions, and mature issues that often arise when studying current events and global issues, we will also discuss some considerations about navigating this in the classroom.

Human Rights Lens

Global events and issues may seem large and abstract for children and even adults. Bellows and Buchanan (2022) advocate for teaching the human

DOI: 10.4324/9781003274148-12

connection of events and issues. Although they focus this approach on teaching about war, we contend that it can and should be used for global issues in general. Learning about the humanity of an issue or event helps individuals better conceptualize it, connect with those impacted, and foster empathy. Furthermore, it can take the emphasis off brutality and refocus it on the event or issue's impact.

Approaching global inquiry through the lens of human rights can help students focus on the people involved in the event or issue of study (Bellows & Buchanan, 2022). The Universal Declaration of Human Rights (UDHR) and the United Nations' Convention on the Rights of the Child (UN CRC) outline the rights of every human. These documents help students focus on the human impact. Furthermore, being familiar with each gives the learner a tool to use throughout global inquiry both in and out of school.

Cultural Context

Culture is an important factor in discussing global issues. Each global issue or event occurs within a particular place and community, oftentimes with a culture that is not the learner's home culture. Sometimes we might be teaching specifically about a place and its people. Other times we inquire into an event occurring within a context where culture is a necessary consideration. Merryfield (2004) advocates for substantive cultural learning, a framework comprised of five pedagogical foci of global educators:

1. Developing Skills in Perspective Consciousness

Perspective consciousness is the ability to understand that the way we interpret events is different from the way others see them because our interpretations are shaped by our beliefs, values, and life experiences. When working with students, begin with developing the understanding that perspectives are different and others have reasons for thinking the way they do. We can do this by beginning in their daily life and asking why someone else might see something differently (e.g., "Why doesn't Leticia want to play that game?"). As perspective consciousness is developed, the skills can be practiced with more complex issues.

2. Using Skills in Recognizing Stereotypes, Exotica, and Cultural Universals

Our students enter the classroom with ideas about others which often reflect misconceptions and stereotypes. When we begin a unit of study, it is important to know what ideas they bring with them so they can be addressed in the teaching. Presenting students with primary sources can help them better understand the culture being studied. From there, they can identify commonalities and differences with their own culture.

Cultural universals can be helpful when learning about another culture. This framework calls for the learner to discuss culture within the context of things we all have in common, such as shelter, relationships, values, and food. Once students identify commonalities and differences, the class can discuss some of the reasons why there are differences. This can be as simple as pointing out how clothing differences might be due to climate or forms of transportation might differ due to local terrain. It is important that students do not adopt a deficit mindset or consider the differences as exotic. Examining the causes for these differences should promote perspective consciousness.

3. Using Primary Sources from Cultures/Regions Under Study

Primary sources come directly from the culture being studied. Just as it is important to read children's books written by a cultural insider, studying a culture calls for resources by and for cultural insiders and not simply those written from an American perspective. Frequently, there are online resources created for the culture being studied that are available for free. There are often museums and organizations that have authentic resources about the culture too. The class might be able to take a virtual field trip or view live webcams to see daily life in that area.

A great way to learn about the culture is to invite insiders into your classrooms. Oftentimes, hearing from a person they have met virtually or face to face can foster perspective consciousness because it is more "real" for the students. There are websites that will connect you with classrooms all over the world. This opens the door to collaborative projects, pen pal–type activities, and live video chats. Furthermore, you may be able to find an educator or individual in the country to present to your class virtually. You may also be able to invite a cultural insider from your own community to come speak to your class.

4. Understanding of the Intersections of Prejudice and Power

Inequities will become apparent when studying global cultures and issues. It is important to have honest discussions of power and prejudice in the classroom. As mentioned earlier, the UDHR and UN CRC can form frameworks to help students process what rights the individuals in question should have, but it is also important to consider the source of the injustice. Students should not leave the lessons thinking others are "dirty" or "poor" but instead understand the challenges, discrimination, and exploitation the society faces. A discussion on child labor or resource exploitation, for example, might require that the teacher develop more background knowledge before teaching the lesson, but it is important that students develop the understanding of how power and prejudice have worked to create inequity.

At the same time, it is important that students develop an understanding of an individual's agency. Whenever possible, find examples of individuals in that community who are working against injustice. Teaching examples of everyday people who are making a difference counteracts the idea that those facing inequities are helpless. Additionally, the last step of inquiry is to act, so encourage your students to take actions supporting those facing injustice.

5. Understanding of Dynamic Change and Increasing Global Interconnectedness

Cultures change and adapt over time. Though standards may allow for a culture to be taught from a historical perspective, students need to understand that a group of people is living in the present day and that their culture is dynamic. For example, teaching about Native Americans and their role in the traditional Thanksgiving story can give students the idea that Native Americans are no longer living or that their culture and daily life are the same as it was in the 1600s. Merryfield (2004) suggests teaching a culture over the course of three generations to show change over time.

The world has also become more interconnected over time. Just within the course of a few decades, cell phones and the internet have connected individuals with people and information all over the world. It is important to explore how the actions of an individual, family, community, or country affect people in other places too.

When teaching about global issues, focusing on a human rights lens and cultural contexts can help students make sense of issues by giving them a framework to work with for school inquiries and when learning about global issues in other spaces.

Content Knowledge

Teacher

Note: Some of the teacher resources may be helpful for students, especially higher-level readers. However, be sure to review all content carefully, as we are recommending them as teacher resources and have not reviewed them for student use.

The Universal Declaration of Human Rights (UDHR) was adopted in 1948 in response to the atrocities of World War II (Universal Declaration of Human Rights, n.d.). This document states 30 rights that all human beings are guaranteed regardless of gender, ethnicity, or nationality. Although it is not legally binding, the UDHR forms the foundation for many countries' laws and policies.

The United Nations Convention on the Rights of the Child (UN CRC) was adopted in 1989 and lays out the rights that children have, adopting the idea that childhood is a protected part of life and lasts up until the child is 18. It is the most widely ratified treaty concerning human rights. (Though note, the United States has not ratified it. The only other country to not ratify it is Somalia.)

When using the UDHR or the UN CRC as a framework, students must first be familiar with the documents and the rights guaranteed therein. In the lesson highlighted in this chapter, the UN CRC is introduced before using it as a lens for the inquiry. Similar activities can be used to introduce the UDHR, or it can be taught in a stand-alone lesson if you

would like to delve into the framework a bit more. It is easy to find cop-
ies of the documents, simplified versions, and infographics outlining the
rights within each through a quick online search. We suggest giving the
students a brief introduction to the document's history and purpose and
then having the students focus on the rights. For example, you might
read a child-friendly or simplified version of the UDHR and ask a few
discussion questions such as the following:

- Which right do you think is the most important? Why?
- Are you surprised by any of the rights listed? Which ones?
- Which one do you think is the biggest issue in your daily life?

The class could also watch one of the numerous videos online or read a
picture book that describes their rights. Approaching the documents in
this manner makes them accessible to most learners and helps students
connect with their own experiences.

As mentioned earlier, a quick online search will turn up a wealth of
resources. In the next section are several online resources and books that
might be helpful for you and your students. Many organizations will also
send you free print resources upon request. We want to caution you to
examine the authors of each source, though, as there are some prominent
resources written by religious organizations. Although those resources
may be strong, using them in a public school classroom might be prob-
lematic. We have excluded those resources in our list; however, some of
the organizations we list might have links to them on their resource lists.

Resources About the Convention on the Rights of the Child

1. **UNICEF, "Convention on the Rights of the Child?" www.unicef.
   org/child-rights-convention**
   This website provides an in-depth summary of the CRC and links
   to even more information. The links at the bottom of the page also
   include educator and student resources.
2. **UN Office of the High Commissioner for Human Rights,
   "The Children's Rights Convention," www.ohchr.org/en/
   instruments-mechanisms/instruments/convention-rights-child**

This website includes the full text of the CRC. An important, formal source but might be difficult for children to read.

3. **UN Office of the High Commissioner for Human Rights, "Committee on the Rights of the Child," www.ohchr.org/en/treaty-bodies/crc**
   This website includes information about the UN Committee on the Rights of the Child. It includes pertinent information about current situations and discussions about children's rights globally.

4. **Allen, JoBeth and Lois Alexander, eds.** *A Critical Inquiry Framework for K–12 Teachers: Lessons and Resources from the U.N. Rights of the Child.* **New York: Teachers College Press, 2013**
   This book describes nine critical inquiry lessons, each centered on an article of the UN CRC.

Resources About Girl's Rights and Issues, Including Education

1. **UN Girls Education Initiative, www.ungei.org**
   UNGEI supports global and national development agendas to reflect emerging concerns on girls' education and gender equality, especially for the most marginalized.

2. **UNICEF Regional Offices and Websites, www.unicef.org/where-we-work**
   This website allows users to browse an alphabetical listing of all the nations and areas where UNICEF is working. There is usually pertinent information about the status of girls' education.

3. **Girl Up, girlup.org/resources/**
   The United Nation Foundation's campaign focusing on adolescent girls. It provides background information, an impact flier, photos, and other media materials. The UN Foundation supports the work of the UN but is not part of it.

4. **Time for School, www.pbs.org/show/time-school**
   An award-winning, 12-year documentary project that "follows seven children – from Afghanistan, Benin, Brazil, India, Japan, Kenya, and Romania – who are struggling to achieve what is not yet a global birth-right – a basic education."

5. **U.S. Department of State, Office of Global Women's Issues**
   www.state.gov/s/gwi/
   This website includes links about US foreign policy towards women's economic development worldwide.
6. **Peace Corps, Global Issues: Gender Equality and Women's Empowerment**
   www.peacecorps.gov/educators/resources/global-issues-gender-equality-and-womens-empowerment/
   This website by the Peace Corps has explanations and sources about gender equality around the world. It is searchable by country.
7. **Plan International's global initiative to end gender inequality**
   http://becauseiamagirl.ca
   This website includes information about programs to promote gender equality globally.
8. **The Coalition for Adolescent Girls, Resources: http://coalitionforadolescentgirls.org/resources-by-topic-2/**
   This website has resources for topics related to girls' equality and empowerment. Topics include girls' education, female genital mutilation, economic engagement, health, and many more.

Resources about Human Rights

1. **Amnesty International, www.amnesty.org/en/**
   This site, especially the education section, offers resources for teachers to build their own background about human rights as well as lesson plans. Furthermore, their blog contains entries about human rights education from teachers around the world.
2. **Human Rights Educators USA (HREUSA), https://hreusa.org/**
   This group is a collaboration of HR educators. There are several classroom resources and lessons designed across grade levels.
3. **Human Rights Watch, www.hrw.org/**
   This site outlines key human rights issues by country and topic. The educational resources section also includes human rights stories written for younger readers.

Students:

Online and Multimedia Resources

1. **CRC child-friendly resources, www.unicef.org/rightsite/484_540.htm**
   A collection of downloadable resources: "Rights for Every Child," "Little Book of Children's Rights and Responsibilities," Child Rights Flier," and so on.

2. **UNICEF Children's Rights Photo Essay/Slideshow, youtu.be/4jiVUND-KJQ**
   This 2 minute video shows photos of children from around the world with captions that cite articles of the CFC (but do not identify where or when each photo was taken). Pleasant piano music plays in the background.

3. **"Girls Left Behind: Girl's Education in Africa," uis.unesco.org/apps/visuali-sations/no-girl-left-behind**
   A catchy online slideshow with informative captions (no music). Related slideshows are at uis.unesco.org/en/visuali-tions.

Trade Books

1. **Ruurs, Margriet.** *My School in the Rain Forest: How Children Attend School Around the World.* **Honesdale, PA: Boyds Mills Press, 2009**
   This is a photo essay book showing how students in different parts of the world get to school.

2. **McCarney, Rosemary with Jen Albaugh and Plan International.** *Because I am a Girl: I Can Change the World.* **Toronto: Second Story Press 2014**
   This book tells the story of several girls working towards an education across the world. It delves into different hardships and barriers girls face when trying to achieve an education.

3. **Trent, Tererai.** *The Girl Who Buried Her Dreams in a Can: A True Story.* **New York: Viking Books for Young Readers, 2015**
   This is a picture book about Dr. Tererai Trent who grew up in Rhodesia where many girls were not educated.

4. **Winter, Jeanette.** *Nasreen's Secret School: A True Story from Afghanistan.* **New York: Beach Lane Books, 2009**

   This book tells the story of a young girl who had to attend a secret school in Afghanistan.

5. **Burningham, J., Daly, N., Paul, K., Boyne, J., & Tennant, D. (2015).** *We Are All Born Free: The Universal Declaration of Human Rights in Pictures.* **Frances Lincoln Children's Books**

   This beautiful picture book illustrates each of the rights in the Universal Declaration of Human Rights. It is very child friendly.

6. **Robinson, M. (2009).** *Every Human Has Rights: A Photographic Declaration for Kids Based on the United Nations Universal Declaration of Human Rights.* **National Geographic**

   This book includes photos to represent each of the rights in the Universal Declaration of Human Rights.

7. **Rocha, R., & Roth, O. (1989).** *The Universal Declaration of Human Rights: An Adaptation for Children.* **United Nations**

   This book includes the rights from the Universal Declaration of Human Rights in child-friendly language and with child-friendly pictures.

8. **Serres, A., & Fronty Aurélia. (2016).** *I Have the Right to Be a Child.* **Groundwood Books**

   This book is a child-friendly version of the Convention on the Rights of the Child. It has child-friendly language and pictures.

Pedagogy

Compelling Question: How can children's right to an education be realized for girls around the world today?

Objectives:

- Students will be able to explain the purpose of the UN CRC and identify the rights it guarantees.
- Students will be able to identify and explain barriers to education that girls face around the world using the framework of the UN CRC.
- Students will be able to discuss ways to address the barriers to education that girls face around the world.

Throughout the lesson, we will reference graphic organizers. The "Inquiry Graphic Organizer" synthesizes the full lesson. It will be used at the beginning of the lesson for the compelling question and initial hypothesis. Then students will return to the Inquiry Graphic Organizer each time they complete a supporting question to record their findings and revised hypothesis. It will also be used when they write their final conclusion. The other graphic organizers, "Supporting Question __ Graphic Organizer," will support student inquiry for each of the supporting questions. As they investigate each question, students will complete the appropriate graphic organizer to record their findings for each source and their revised hypothesis. We find it helpful to fill in parts of each graphic organizer with the questions and sources before giving them to students. The graphic organizers for this lesson are provided at the end of the chapter.

Introduction

Activating Background Knowledge

There are two parts to activating background knowledge for this lesson. The first focuses on the UN CRC in general and the second on the right to education more specifically.

Part 1: UN CRC

- Teachers should pose the question "What rights do children around the world have? What rights do you have as someone under 18?"
- Allow students 5–10 minutes to reflect on these and begin to write a response.
- Either provide a graphic organizer or have students create one, which has two columns:

Table 10.1 Children's Rights in the CRC

The Rights Children Have	My Thoughts and Connections

- Teachers should play the photo essay published by UNICEF (listed earlier in student content).
- As students view the photo essay, ask them to fill in the two columns notes with their learning and responses.
- Teachers should have a brief discussion about the students' reactions to the photo essay.
- Teachers should post the following questions for students to answer while looking at the two separate infographics:
  - What is the UN CRC?
  - Who wrote it? Why?
  - Who enforces it?
  - Who does it apply to?
  - What has its impact been?
- Teachers will show the online infographic "What is the CRC?" (listed earlier in student content), which outlines the categories that organize the rights as well as the monitoring of rights.
- Teachers should show "Celebrating the CRC" (listed earlier in student content), another online infographic, which helps students understand the organization of the document as well as some of its impacts and the ongoing issues.
- Teachers should have a brief discussion of the questions in the previous section after students have looked at both infographics.
- Teachers should reiterate that the rights defined in the UN CRC are for all children under the age of 18 regardless of race, gender, or religion. If the students continue to have questions or the teacher would like students to gain a deeper understanding of the document, the full text as well as other resources are easily accessible online.

Part 2: Right to Education

- Teachers will show Malala's acceptance speech for the Harvard Foundation's 2013 Peter J. Gomes Humanitarian of the Year Award (www.youtube.com/watch?v=e1tOe4SKbLU). The speech references the barriers Malala faced when seeking her education and also notes the experiences of girls in several contexts around the world.
- After viewing the video of the Harvard speech, the teacher should write on the board this quote from Malala's Nobel Prize acceptance

speech: "I tell my story, not because it is unique, but because it is not. It is the story of many girls" (Yousafzai, 2014).

- Teachers should tell the students that they will begin to investigate the barriers that stand in the way as girls around the world seek to fulfill their right to education. Although they will be learning about the issues in the country, rather than specific girls in each context, students should consider what the stories of the girls in each of the countries they explore might be like.

Introduce Compelling Question

At this point in the lesson, don't discuss the compelling question much. Introduce the question and remind students that the goal for this lesson is to answer this question. Invite them to silently consider the question for a minute or two. Remind students to think about what they already know that might help them to answer this question.

Hypothesis

After thinking about the compelling question, have students write their initial hypothesis. Remind them that it is always good to provide evidence about their thinking but also to remember that this is their initial hypothesis, so it might be a guess at this point. As they continue in the lesson, they will gather more evidence to support their thinking.

Instructional Procedures

For this inquiry, there are seven stations, focusing on different topics that can impact girls' education across the globe. Each station includes supporting questions for students to answer. Remember, after students visit each station, they should revisit and refine their hypothesis. Additionally, some of these stations may only be appropriate for older students. You can choose which stations are appropriate for your students.

Barrier 1: Child Marriage
Supporting Question 1: How does forcing young girls into marriage keep them from attaining an education?

Sources:

www.girlsnotbrides.org/about-child-marriage/
This is a video about ending child marriage in Guatemala.
www.girlsnotbrides.org/learning-resources/child-marriage-and-
    education/
The website includes information on how child marriage impact education.

Barrier 2: Refugees
Supporting Question 2: Why is it important for refugees to continue
    their education? What are barriers that stand in the way?

Sources:

https://girlup.org/voices/the-importance-of-education-for-refugee-girls
This has several first-person stories about the importance of education
    for refugee girls.

Barrier 3: Periods/General Health
Supporting Question 3: How can starting menstruation create barriers
    for education?

Sources:

www.globalcitizen.org/en/content/menstrual-hygiene-day-education/
This website includes information about how periods can keep girls out
    of school when they can't afford menstrual products.
www.unicefusa.org/stories/how-good-menstrual-hygiene-keeps-girls-
    learning/34632
This website has similar information about how lack of access to hygiene
    products impacts girls' education.
https://girlup.org/voices/on-world-menstrual-hygiene-day-meeting-my-
    girlhero
This website also includes information about lack of access to hygiene
    products but is specifically about India.

Barrier 4: Gender Violence
Supporting Question 4: What is gender violence, and how can it impact
    a girls' education?

Sources:

www.ungei.org/blog-post/changing-minds-and-taking-action-end-
    gender-violence-schools
This is about two programs (one in India and one in Brazil), which work
    with children to end gender stereotypes and violence.
www.ungei.org/sites/default/files/Education-unions-take-action-to-
    end-school-related-gender-based-violence-2018-eng.pdf
This has a good overview of what gender violence in schools is and how
    some countries are fighting against it. It is longer but includes a lot
    of graphs, quotes, pictures, and so on.

Barrier 5: Climate Change
Supporting Question 5: How does climate change impact girls' educa-
    tion? How does girls' education impact climate change?

Sources:

www.brookings.edu/blog/education-plus-development/2021/02/10/
    why-is-girls-education-important-for-climate-action/
This website provides information about how climate change impacts
    girls' education and also how making sure girls have access to edu-
    cation can help slow climate change.
https://malala.org/newsroom/malala-fund-publishes-report-on-
    climate-change-and-girls-education
This is a report explaining the connections between climate change and
    girls' access to education.

Barrier 6: Economics
Supporting Question 6: How do gender roles impact girls' access to educa-
    tion? How can girls' access to education impact a country's economics?

Sources:

www.ungei.org/news/counting-zeros
This website is about how much it costs (economically, socially, etc.) to
    not educate women.
www.unicef.org/press-releases/girls-spend-160-million-more-hours-
    boys-doing-household-chores-everyday

This talks about the inequity of how many household chores girls typically have instead of boys. It addresses how hours of unpaid labor impact girls' economic growth.

Barrier 7: Gender Stereotypes
Supporting Question 7: How do stereotypes impact girls' education?

Sources:

www.enspired.net/en/inspiration/international-womens-day-cambodia-
get-rid-gender-stereotypes
This is a video from a lesson in Cambodia against gender stereotypes. It
mostly focuses on toys (ball vs. doll) but also talks about homosexuality.
www.ungei.org/publication/challenging-gender-bias-and-stereotypes-
and-through-education
This is a fact sheet about gender stereotypes.

Conclusion

In the final conclusion, students have an opportunity to discuss their responses to the supporting questions and their final answer to the compelling question.

- Teachers should gather the entire class together again, and each group should display their answer to the supporting question for each barrier.
- Teachers should guide a discussion about the potential answers to the compelling question. The discussion should address the supporting questions for each individual country and how it contributes to their answer. Students should provide evidence for their responses from the provided resources and the UN CRC.
- At the conclusion of the discussion, each group should once again write or revise their answer to the compelling question according to what they learned through the discussion.

Optional Extension

One recommendation is to have students create a newscast reporting on the topic of girls' education. A second possible extension could be students working together to create a PSA to use as a launch for a school-wide awareness campaign. A third possibility would be to create infographics to share at school or in the community.

Adaptability and Differentiation

Early Childhood

When adapting this lesson for early childhood, it is important to use the child-friendly versions of the UN CRC. It might also be helpful to complete the stations as a whole class and not in small groups. Finally, younger children may not be mature enough for every station. But completing the stations on refugees, climate change, and economics will teach them about some barriers to education that girls face around the world.

Middle Level

All stations may be appropriate for middle grades, but you, as teachers, know your students best. It might be beneficial to complete some stations in small groups and others as a whole class. Reading levels of some sources may also need to be adjusted.

Students with Special Needs

Although the task is planned as small-group station work, teachers may decide a different format would be more beneficial for their students. For example, the whole class may examine each barrier together and work as a large group to explore the resources and answer the supporting questions. The teacher may decide, instead, to assign individual barriers to small groups. In this case, students would engage with their small group to examine a single barrier. Then they would present their findings and the answers to their supporting questions to the whole class. Finally, the large group would collaborate to answer the compelling question. Additionally, the reading material can be varied for reading level and students can use assistive technology to have texts read aloud, if needed. Completing the stations in small groups can also allow for each group to get a different set of texts. Additionally, the teacher can provide varying levels of support to each group according to their needs or the station they are working on.

Inquiry Graphic Organizer

Compelling Question:
How can children's right to an education be realized for girls around the world today?

Hypothesis:

Supporting Question 1: How does forcing young girls into marriage keep them from attaining an education?	Supporting Question 2: Why is it important for refugees to continue their education? What are barriers that stand in the way?	Supporting Question 3: How can starting menstruation create barriers for education?	Supporting Question 4: What is gender violence and how can it impact a girls' education?	Supporting Question 5: How does climate change impact girls' education? How does girls' education impact climate change?	Supporting Question 6: How do gender roles impact girls' access to education? How can girls' access to education impact a country's economics?	Supporting Question 7: How do stereotypes impact girls' education?
Findings:	Findings:	Findings:	Findings:	Findings:	Findings:	Findings:
Revised Hypothesis:	Revised Hypothesis:	Revised Hypothesis:	Revised Hypothesis:	Revised Hypothesis:	Revised Hypothesis:	Revised Hypothesis:

Final Conclusion (should answer CQ and use evidence):

Additional Notes:

Figure 10.1 "How can children's right to an education be realized for girls around the world today?" Inquiry Graphic Organizer

Barrier 1 Graphic Organizer

Barrier 1: Child Marriage
Supporting Question: How does forcing young girls into marriage keep them from attaining an education?

Source 1: https://www.girlsnotbrides.org/about-child-marriage/	Source 2: https://www.girlsnotbrides.org/learning-resources/child-marriage-and-education/

Findings:	Findings:

Revised Hypothesis (Use evidence from your findings):

Figure 10.2 "How does forcing young girls into marriage keep them from attaining an education?" Barrier 1 Graphic Organizer

Barrier 2 Graphic Organizer

Barrier 2: Refugees

Supporting Question: Why is it important for refugees to continue their education? What are barriers that stand in the way?

Source: https://girlup.org/voices/the-importance-of-education-for-refugee-girls

Findings:

Revised Hypothesis (Use evidence from your findings):

Figure 10.3 "Why is it important for refugees to continue their education? What are barriers that stand in the way?" Barrier 2 Graphic Organizer

Barrier 3 Graphic Organizer

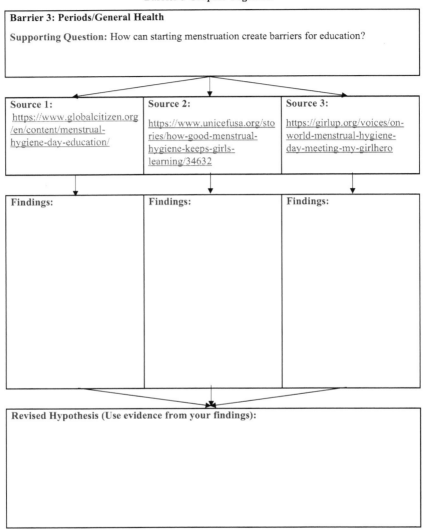

Figure 10.4 "How can starting menstruation create barriers for education?" Barrier 3 Graphic Organizer

Barrier 4 Graphic Organizer

Barrier 4: Gender Violence

Supporting Question: What is gender violence and how can it impact a girls' education?

Source 1: https://www.ungei.org/blog-post/changing-minds-and-taking-action-end-gender-violence-schools	Source 2: https://www.ungei.org/sites/default/files/Education-unions-take-action-to-end-school-related-gender-based-violence-2018-eng.pdf
Findings:	**Findings:**

Revised Hypothesis (Use evidence from your findings):

Figure 10.5 "What is gender violence and how can it impact a girls' education?" Barrier 4 Graphic Organizer

Barrier 5 Graphic Organizer

Barrier 5: Climate Change

Supporting Question: How does climate change impact girls' education? How does girls' education impact climate change?

Source 1:	Source 2:
https://www.brookings.edu/blog/education-plus-development/2021/02/10/why-is-girls-education-important-for-climate-action/	https://malala.org/newsroom/malala-fund-publishes-report-on-climate-change-and-girls-education

Findings:	Findings:

Revised Hypothesis (Use evidence from your findings):

Figure 10.6 "How does climate change impact girls' education? How does girls' education impact climate change?" Barrier 5 Graphic Organizer

Barrier 6 Graphic Organizer

Barrier 6: Economics
Supporting Question: How do gender roles impact girls' access to education? How can girls' access to education impact a country's economics?

Source 1: https://www.ungei.org/news/counting-zeros	**Source 2:** https://www.unicef.org/press-releases/girls-spend-160-million-more-hours-boys-doing-household-chores-everyday
Findings:	**Findings:**

Revised Hypothesis (Use evidence from your findings):

Figure 10.7 "How do gender roles impact girls' access to education? How can girls' access to education impact a country's economics?" Barrier 6 Graphic Organizer

Barrier 7 Graphic Organizer

Barrier 7: Gender Stereotypes

Supporting Question: How do stereotypes impact girls' education?

Source 1:

https://www.enspired.net/en/inspiration/international-womens-day-cambodia-get-rid-gender-stereotypes

Source 2:

https://www.ungei.org/publication/challenging-gender-bias-and-stereotypes-and-through-education

---

Findings:

Findings:

Revised Hypothesis (Use evidence from your findings):

Figure 10.8 "How do stereotypes impact girls' education?" Barrier 7 Graphic Organizer

References

Bellows, E., & Buchanan, L. B. (2022). Approaching the teaching of war in the elementary classroom with text sets. *Social Studies and the Young Learner, 34*(4), 3–12.

Merryfield, M. M. (2004). Elementary students in substantive culture learning. *Social Education, 68*(4), 270–274.

The United Nations. Convention on the Rights of the Child. (1989). *Treaty series 1577*. United Nations. www.ohchr.org/EN/ProfessionalInterest/Pages/CRC.aspx

Universal Declaration of Human Rights. (n.d.). *Amnesty international.* Retrieved May 19, 2022, from www.amnesty.org/en/what-we-do/universal-declaration-of-human-rights/

Yousafzai, M. (2014). Nobel lecture. *Nobel Media.* Retrieved November 10, 2017. www.nobelprize.org/nobel_prizes/peace/laureates/2014/yousafzai-lecture_en.html

INDEX